rororo sprachen
Herausgegeben von Ludwig Moos

Selbst wer im Business English ziemlich geübt ist, hat mitunter Schwierigkeiten beim Lesen der englischsprachigen Wirtschaftspresse mit ihren Kürzeln und Fachbegriffen. *How to Read the Business Press* baut die Brücke zum Verständnis. Jedes Kapitel erschließt einen informativen, mitunter auch amüsanten Beitrag Schritt für Schritt: vom lockeren Dialog, der in das jeweilige Thema einführt, über vergleichende Übungen zur Wirtschaftssprache bis zum erläuterten Originaltext. So erwerben Sie mit einer ausgefeilten Methode Sachkenntnis und Sprachkenntnis zugleich. Ein spezielles Training der Lesetechnik hilft Ihnen überdies, sich Wirtschaftsartikel schneller und mit größerem Gewinn anzueignen.

Dr. René Bosewitz ist Native Speaker und bereitet in einer deutschen Zweigstelle der London Chamber of Commerce Firmenangehörige auf einschlägige sprachliche Prüfungen vor. Er trainiert zudem seit vielen Jahren Manager aus Banken und Industrie in Business English. Mit Robert Kleinschroth hat er bei rororo sprachen *Joke Your Way Through English Grammar* (8572) und *Joke by Joke to Conservation* (8795) veröffentlicht.

Robert Kleinschroth unterrichtet Englisch am Gymnasium und an der Universität Heidelberg. Er hat zwanzig Jahre Praxis in der Erwachsenenbildung und leitete fünfzehn Jahre lang die Sprachabteilung eines Großunternehmens. Robert Kleinschroth hat zusammen mit Dieter Maupai *La Grammaire en s'amusant* (8714) verfaßt und außerdem *La Conservation en s'amusant* (8873) sowie *Sprachen lernen* (9140) und *Neues Lernen mit dem Computer* (9841) geschrieben.

In der Reihe Business English sind von beiden Autoren außerdem erschienen: *Manage in English* (60137), *Better than the Boss* (60138), *How to Phone Effectively* (60139), *Drop Them a Line* (60261, mit Bryan Hemming), *Test Your Management Skills* (60260), *Get Through at Meetings* (60262), *Let's Go International* (60267), *Check Your Language Level* (60268), *Business English from A to Z* (60269, mit Bryan Hemming), *The Way Things Work* (60369) und *Small Talk for Big Business* (60577).

ROBERT KLEINSCHROTH / RENÉ BOSEWITZ

HOW TO READ THE BUSINESS PRESS

BUSINESS ENGLISH

FÜR DIE AKTUELLE INFORMATION

Rowohlt
rororo

Wir danken Frau Ortrud Grimm vielmals für ihre Hilfe bei der Erstellung des Manuskripts. Ohne sie hätten wir es wohl nicht geschafft.

Originalausgabe
Veröffentlicht im Rowohlt Taschenbuch Verlag GmbH,
Reinbek bei Hamburg, Oktober 1998

Umschlaggestaltung Barbara Hanke
(Illustration Cathrin Günther)
Layout Anne Drude und Alexander Urban
Satz OCR-A und Stone PostScript,
QuarkXPress 3.32
(Dolev 800)
Druck und Bindung Clausen & Bosse, Leck
Printed in Germany
ISBN 3 499 60506 6

Inhalt

Themes	page
1 The battle for the beaches	10
2 Euromania	22
3 When jokes backfire	30
4 Supermarkets the American way	40
5 Prince joins battle for language	48
6 How to kick-start Germany's economy	56
7 Destress in salt water	64
8 The Elk test	72
9 The price of beauty	80
10 BSE or the mad cow disease	90
11 Buba and the Euro	98
12 Nike versus Adidas	106
13 Transparent man	115
14 Motorcar misery	125
15 The best meals in the skies	135
16 Bullying bosses and the Nanny State	143
17 Shop around the clock	152
18 Making both ends meet	161
19 Telebusiness from Ireland	169
20 Between bulls and bears	178

Reading skills	
1 Understanding headlines	17
2 Skim to get an overview	29
3 Scan to get an answer to a question	38
4 Grasping the central idea	39
5 Guessing the meaning of unknown words	89
6 Facts about speed reading	114
7 Reading with your fingers	124
8 About hand and mouth	134
9 Vertical scanning for meaning	142
10 Reading and mind mapping	188

Appendix	
A: Headline words	190
B: Advertisement abbreviations	193
C: Word-building	194
Key to the exercises	198

Sie haben ein Lern- und Lesebuch aufgeschlagen. Es enthält zwanzig ausgewählte Originalartikel aus der Welt der Wirtschaft und zehn Minilektionen zur Verbesserung Ihrer Lesetechnik. Kurze *jokes* und humorvolle Zitate zum Thema sorgen dafür, daß alles besser rutscht, obwohl unsere Artikel keineswegs trocken sind, sondern amüsant und informativ zugleich. Da lesen Sie über Bestrebungen, eine Euronorm für Christbäume durchzusetzen, über eine Fluggesellschaft, die auf dem Boden bleibt und sich aufs Kochen spezialisiert, von neuen Entspannungstechniken für Manager und der Pille gegen Fettpolster. Auch die Schweizer BSE-Kuh Anita und der Elchtest fehlen nicht.
Wir tun auch etwas für Ihre Lesetechnik. Sie werden lernen, die Wirtschaftspresse schneller und mit größerem Gewinn zu lesen. Der normale Leser liest einen deutschen Text mit rund 250 Wörtern pro Minute. Er bräuchte für ein Buch mit 90 000 Wörtern sechs Stunden, der Geübte nur drei Stunden. Zeit ist Geld. In der Fremdsprache geht es natürlich nicht ganz so schnell. Aber selbst wenn Sie sich von 100 bis 150 Wörtern auf die doppelte Geschwindigkeit steigern, hat sich das Buch für Sie gelohnt.
Trainieren Sie nach unseren zehn Anleitungen (*Boost your reading skills*) zum Schnell- und Intensivlesen, zum Erschließen unbekannter Wörter, zum schnellen Erfassen des Wesentlichen oder zum Entschlüsseln der oft rätselhaften Schlagzeilen. Diese Techniken werden Ihnen auch beim Lesen von Fachtexten aller Art nützlich sein.
Jedes Kapitel ist einem Artikel gewidmet, auf den Sie drei Übungsbatterien in kurzen Schritten systematisch vorbereiten. Sie werden feststellen, daß ein bestimmter Wortschatz sich immer wieder, unabhängig vom Thema, wiederholt und sich durch unsere abwechslungsreichen, kurzen Übungen einprägt. Dies wird Ihnen die Lektüre der englischsprachigen Presse auch in Zukunft erheblich erleichtern. Die Lösungen zu den Tests verschafft Ihnen wie immer der *key* im Anhang. Der Wegweiser gibt Ihnen einen Überblick über den Aufbau der Kapitel.

Viel Spaß bei der Lektüre!

Wegweiser

⊛ Our story

Sie lesen einen kurzen Dialog, der Sie in die Thematik einführt. Dabei begegnen Ihnen bereits viele der *keywords* des späteren Artikels.

W Word watch

Sie lernen den neuen Wortschatz, indem Sie unsere Übungsaufgaben lösen. Alle Übungen sind kurz und für die Leser gedacht, die nicht stundenlang die üblichen Lehrbücher studieren können. In der ersten Übungsbatterie vertiefen und festigen Sie den Wortschatz, der sowohl im Dialog als auch im Artikel vorkommt.

1. Scanning for keywords
Sie überfliegen (*scanning*) den Dialog und versuchen die Schlüsselwörter herauszufiltern, die zu vorgegebenen Wortschatzerklärungen passen.

2. In other words
Diese Übung trainiert Ihr Gedächtnis. Wir geben Ihnen Sätze aus dem Dialog, die wir leicht verändert haben. Sie sollen sich an den genauen Wortlaut erinnern. Dabei erweitern Sie Ihren Wortschatz und werden den folgenden Artikel leichter verstehen.

3. Complete the business idioms
Hier werden nützliche *business idioms*, die sowohl im Dialog als auch im Artikel vorkommen, erweitert und variiert.

P Word power

Die zweite Übungsbatterie bereitet das Textverständnis vor, erweitert und vertieft Ihren Wortschatz. Zuvor sollten Sie aber den Artikel einmal gelesen haben. Weniger Fortgeschrittene werden die Vokabelliste Word aid zu Rate ziehen und dann die Übungen machen. Versuchen Sie es aber immer zuerst einmal ohne Vokabelhilfe.

1. Wordfinder's corner
Ihren Wortschatz können Sie vervielfachen, wenn Sie zu einem bekannten Verb wie zum Beispiel *compete* die Substantive *competitor, competition, competitiveness* ableiten können. Lernen Sie zu einem Ausdruck wie

reduce costs das Gegenteil *increase costs* oder das gleichbedeutende *raise costs* mit. Da sich in Zeitungsartikeln der Wortschatz wiederholt, werden Sie die Regeln bald anwenden können. Die Lernpsychologie hat bewiesen, daß durch solche Übungen der Wortschatz flexibler und einprägsamer wird.

2. Words in context
Sie versuchen nun, Ihre Lösungen in den richtigen Zusammenhang zu bringen. Der Wortschatz prägt sich dadurch nachhaltiger ein.

3. Guesswork
Man muß nicht alle Wörter eines Texts kennen, um ihn zu verstehen. Viele lassen sich aus dem Zusammenhang erschließen. An das Erschließen können Sie sich anhand dieser Übung gewöhnen. Dazu haben wir Ihnen eine kleine Anleitung gegeben (siehe auch *Boost your reading skills: Guessing the meaning of unknown words*).

! Digesting the article

Nach nochmaliger Lektüre des Artikels können Sie Ihr Leseverständnis prüfen. Je nach Artikel helfen Ihnen unter anderen folgende Übungstypen:

1. Did you get the message?
Sie kreuzen an, ob unsere Behauptungen zum Inhalt richtig oder falsch sind. Vorsicht, es sieht leichter aus, als es ist. Auch hier finden Sie eine kurze Anleitung (siehe *Boost your reading skills: Grasping the central idea*), die sich auf viele Artikel anwenden läßt.

2. Note-taking practice
Manchmal fordern wir Sie auf, Notizen zu machen beziehungsweise zu vervollständigen. So weit die wichtigsten Übungen.

Der Anhang

Der Anhang ist vielleicht wichtiger als ein 21. oder 22. Kapitel. Er enthält wichtige Informationen, auf die Sie bei Ihrer weiteren Lektüre immer wieder zurückgreifen können.

Appendix A: Headline words
Hier erhalten Sie einen Schlüssel zu den oft rätselhaften englischen Schlagzeilen. Journalisten verwenden dafür kurze dynamische oder emotionale Wörter. Wir geben Ihnen eine Liste dieser typischen Wörter an die Hand, die Ihnen in Zeitungen immer wieder begegnen werden.

Appendix B: Abbreviations
Wer hätte nicht schon mal gerätselt, was die vielen Abkürzungen im Annonceteil bedeuten. In der Fremdsprache hilft meist weder Raten noch Wörterbuch. Schlagen Sie bei uns nach.

Appendix C: Word-building
Wer weiß, wie der Engländer Wörter bildet, kann viele unbekannte Wörter aus dem Zusammenhang erschließen und sein Vokabular erheblich erweitern. Wir haben Ihnen deshalb die wichtigsten Wortbausteine zusammengestellt.

Key to the exercises
Hier finden Sie die Lösungen zu den *tasks*.

The battle for the beaches

OUR STORY: Deck-chair dispute

THE ARTICLE: Britain steals a march in battle for the beaches

Whet your appetite

The last time Britain went into Europe with any degree of success was on 6 June 1944. Since then strategies have changed. British tour operators are landing on our shores to buy hotels and beaches in bulk thus offering lower prices for holidaymakers. This has caused bad feelings amongst Europeans.

Time for a smile

Traveller: "Excuse me, do you have a room for tonight?"
Hotel owner: "Certainly, sir. It'll be fifteen pounds a night. Or I can let you have a room for only five pounds, if you make your own bed."
Traveller: "I'll take the five-pound room."
Hotel owner: "Right, I'll just go and fetch the wood, the hammer, the nails and the other materials for the bed."

⊛ Deck-chair dispute

On a German beach. Mick Disney (**M**) from Nottingham is out early to sunbathe. Klaus Keller (**K**) is not amused.

M: Typical! These Germans reserve chairs in bulk. Okay, I'll throw this towel on the sand and sit here myself. That'll trigger off some comments when they come back. (*Five minutes later*)
K: He, Sie, haben Sie mein Tuch auf den Boden geschmissen?
M: Sorry, mate, I don't understand your lingo. Do you speak English?
K: Yes, of course. I passed my, what do you say, Abitur?
M: Boasting about qualifications! Actually, I put your towel on the ground. It was lying on a chair.
K: Yes, but perhaps you misunderstood. With the towel I was telling other people that the chair belonged to me.
M: Oh, I see. You've bought the chair, have you?
K: No, no, no! I wanted people to know that I was here first.
M: Oh, I understand. You snapped up the chair at 6 o'clock this morning. But you weren't here when I arrived. It's okay that the first to arrive gets the chair. But you went away.
K: But it is normal.
M: Maybe it's normal for you mate, but not for the rest of the world.
K: We are in Germany and ...
M: (*interrupting*) You're living from your tourists and they have different ways, or don't you like their money?
K: Money is not important for me.
M: Okay, at least we've agreed on that. Look, if you want to battle about chairs, do it by yourself. Here, take the seat. I'll be going.
K: No, no, no. Keep it. It's no problem. Where are you staying?
M: Well, I'm staying at the Zur Rose Hotel. It's really cheap.
K: Cheap? I'm in the same hotel. Their prices are cut-throat. They charged me £400 for a two-week package tour.
M: Well, I've paid £250 to stay there for two weeks. I guess your tour-operators aren't efficient enough to cut their prices to the bone.
K: We have the most efficient tour operators in the world.
M: Hmm! Okay, you go on paying more for things, if you want to. I must say you're efficient at snapping up chairs anyway.
K: Everybody would do the same.
M: Then I'm a nobody. Here, take the chair, I'm off.

Word watch

Task 1: Scanning for keywords

Find the words that have almost the same meaning.

an all inclusive holiday *p . . . . . . t . . .*
travel agency *t . . . o . . . .*
very low prices *c . . - . . . . . . prices*

Task 2: In other words

Remember what they said in the dialogue?

These Germans reserve chairs *in great numbers.*	These Germans reserve chairs ....
That'll *spark off* some comments when they come back.	That'll .... some comments when they come back.
If you want to *fight* about chairs, do it by yourself.	If you want to .... about chairs, do it by yourself.
We have the *best* tour operators in the world.	We have the most .... tour operators in the world.
You're efficient at *reserving* chairs anyway.	You're efficient at .... chairs anyway.

Task 3: Complete the business idioms

Where do these words fit in?

snap trigger cut bring

Ladies and Gentlemen,
We'd hoped our advertising campaign would .... *off* an enormous public response and that smokers would .... *up* our fat-burning, green cigar. As you know this has not been the case and we were forced to .... *down* the price. Let's take this product off the market to .... our losses.

Time for a smile

What you should not say to a German

At the swimming pool: That's my towel.
At the Robinson Club: You're lying on my deck-chair.

P Word power

Task 4: Wordfinder's corner

verb	noun	noun	adjective
....	penetration	....	efficient
....	operators	....	cheap
....	competition	....	identical

Task 5: Guesswork

Read the following article without looking at the wordlist. Then come back and guess what the words in *italics* mean.

1. Mick Disney is out early to sunbathe.
   A. tan **B.** jog **C.** train
2. British tour operators triggered a *shake-up* of the travel industry.
   A. cocktail **B.** meeting **C.** reformation
3. The UK *boasts* the largest travel companies.
   A. rühmt sich **B.** beherrscht **C.** gründet
4. Industry *lore* has it that companies make their profit from duty-free sales.
   A. wisdom **B.** rules **C.** know-how
5. The UK market leaders have made *incursions* into Germany.
   A. attacks **B.** attempts **C.** raids
6. Continental tour operators had *gambled* that their travellers would not accept the more *cramped surroundings* of a UK charter aircraft.
   A. expected **A.** narrow rows of seats
   B. known **B.** overcrowded planes
   C. risked **C.** limited capacity

Britain steals a march in battle for the beaches

Germans and the British traditionally have a stressful relationship on holiday together as they battle over the prime beach spots to tan their pale northern European torsos. Now British tour operators have landed on the German beaches in a big way, triggering a shake-up of the travel industry.

Consolidation in the German market is being driven by the threat of competition from abroad, notably from the UK which boasts the largest travel companies and the most efficient charter airlines. UK charters such as Britannia and Airtours fill 95 per cent of the seats on each flight compared with 75 per cent on German rivals such as LTU and Hapag Lloyd. The larger scale of the UK tour operators allows them to cut hotel prices to the bone by buying in bulk.

In contrast to the cut-throat competition in the British market – industry lore has it that companies make their profit from duty-free sales to the last three rows of a charter flight – competition in Germany has also been limited by the complex web of cross-shareholdings which fragment the market and frustrate innovation.

UK tour operators have meanwhile been busy snapping up businesses on the continent to press home their competitive advantage, which has allowed them to offer identical packages 30 per cent cheaper than German companies. Thomson and Airtours, the UK market leaders, already control the Scandinavian market and have made incursions into Germany and Belgium.

Continental tour operators had gambled that their travellers would not accept the more cramped surroundings of a UK charter aircraft. However, the penetration of the UK companies suggests that their price advantage is crucial, particularly in attracting those from less well-heeled parts of Germany.

Doug Cameron, The European, 9–15 March 1998

Time for a smile: Murphy's laws about flying

The distance to the gate is inversely proportional to the time available to catch your flight.

As soon as the stewardess serves the coffee, the airliner encounters turbulence.

When the plane you are on is late, the plane you want to transfer to is on time.

Digesting the article

Task 6: Scanning for figures

Use the scanning reading skills (*Boost your reading skills 3*, page 38.) and complete the table.

What percentage of the seats do UK charters fill on each tour? ... %
What percentage of the seats do German charters fill on each tour? ... %
By what percentage are UK operators cheaper than German companies? ... %

Task 7: Guided note-taking practice

The British travel industry is a danger for German operators because

1. British travel companies are the ....
2. British charter airlines are the ....
3. Competition in Britain is ....
4. Competition in Germany is ....
5. British charters fill ....
6. They buy hotel rooms ....
7. They offer package tours ....
8. The price advantage is ....

Word aid

abroad	Ausland
attack	Angriff
attempt	Versuch
battle	kämpfen, Kampf
beef up	aufmöbeln
boast	hier: stolz sein auf, sich rühmen
bulk, buy in ~	in großem Stil einkaufen
catch one's flight	sein Flugzeug erreichen
compared with	verglichen mit
competition	Wettbewerb
competitive advantage	Wettbewerbsvorteil
cramped surroundings	hier: enge Platzverhältnisse

crucial	entscheidend, kritisch
cut-throat competition	mörderischer Wettbewerb
deck-chair	Liegestuhl
degree of success	hier: Aussicht auf Erfolg
dispute	Streit
efficient	tüchtig, rationell, effizient
encounter turbulence	in Turbulenzen geraten
fragment the market	den Markt fragmentieren
gamble	spekulieren
gate	Flugsteig
grasp	erfassen, verstehen
incursion	Eindringen, Raubzug
lore	Wissen; Überlieferung
march	hier: Marsch
mate	Kamerad, Kumpel
off , I'm ~	ich gehe, ich bin schon weg
operator	Unternehmer
penetration	Eindringen
press home an advantage	einen Vorteil energisch ausnutzen
prime beach spots	beste Strandplätze
raid	Vorstoß, Überfall, Razzia
scale	Maßstab
shake-up	Aufrütteln
snap something up	sich etwas schnappen
spark off	auslösen
stressful relationship	gespannte Beziehung
suggest	hier: nahelegen
surroundings	Umgebung
tan	sonnenbaden, sich bräunen
threat	Drohung
towel	Handtuch
trigger off	auslösen
web	Netz
well-heeled	gut betucht

✔ Boost your reading skills 1: Understanding headlines

Understanding newspaper *headlines* is a problem for learners of English because a headline writer writes in a tricky way. He must keep three things in mind.

Titel, Überschrift

- First, he must *attract* the interest of the readers and encourage them to go on reading. So he tries to give his headline a dramatic, spectacular or *witty* quality.
- Second, he must do this in a very *limited space*. That is why he leaves out words that are *unnecessary* and chooses the shortest possible words.
- Third, he must give the reader some idea of what the article is about. The title must therefore *be to the point*. Once the rules and the key words have been understood it is no problem to *guess* the meaning of a lot of headlines.

auf sich lenken
geistreich
begrenzter Platz
unnötig
treffend sein
erraten

1. The *choice* of words: Short ones instead of long ones

Wahl

SALES BOOMING

Sales figures are increasing / rising *considerably*

beträchtlich

'Boom' is shorter than *'increase'* and more dynamic than 'rise'. We will give you a list of the most frequently used short words and their meanings in Appendix A.

zunehmen

2. *Abbreviations* where possible

Abkürzungen

EU MPs ON MAASTRICHT

Members of the European Parliament discuss the Maastricht *treaty*

Vertrag

You'll find a list of abbreviations in Appendix B.

3. Style: *Images* instead of ideas

Bilder

FACTORY BLAZE
A big fire at a factory got out of control

Fabrik

'Blaze' is more descriptive than 'big fire'; sensational words *instead of* neutral ones.

anstatt

SALES SKY-ROCKETING
Sales are increasing or booming

'Sky-rocket' is a more emotional and dramatic way of expressing this idea.

4. Grammar striptease

The little words like articles (a, an, the), prepositions (in, on), conjunctions (but, and, while) and forms of 'to be' (is, are, was, were) are often left out. That is why some headlines *consist of nouns* and verbs only.

bestehen aus Substantiven

VW MANAGER SACKED
A manager of VW was *sacked*

entlassen, feuern

VW'S BILLION ROLLS ROYCE *BID*
VW company has offered 1.5 billion marks to buy Rolls-Royce

Angebot

Sometimes prepositions cannot be left out:

LOPEZ IN INDUSTRIAL SPYING
Mr Lopez was *involved in* industrial *espionage*

beteiligt; Spionage

KOHL RAPPED BY TURKEY'S PM
The Prime Minister of Turkey sharply criticised Germany's Chancellor Kohl

5. Present instead of past

The verb system is simplified. The simple present tense is used to describe something happening in the present or the past.

BLAZE KILLS 22
22 people were killed by a fire

Feuersbrunst

6. The forms of 'to be' are left out

The present *progressive tense* (-ing form) is sometimes used to express that something is developing. It has an active meaning. The past participle has a passive meaning.

Verlaufsform

WALL STREET SKY-ROCKETING
Prices of *stocks* are rising dramatically on Wall Street

Aktien

GM EXECUTIVE *JAILED*
A General Motor's executive was / has been imprisoned

hinter Gitter bringen

7. Future time

The infinitive with 'to' is used to talk about the future.

CLINTON TO VISIT AFRICAN STATES
President Bill Clinton is going to visit African states

8. Playing with the language

Journalists like to make use of cultural *allusions* or associations ranging from the latest TV show to *quotations* from the Bible. They also tend to play with the meaning and the sound of words.

Anspielungen

Zitate

A BEAR AMID THE BULLS

Task 8: Skimming exercise (see page 29)

Match the headlines and the articles without looking at the wordlist.

1. A BEAR AMID THE BULLS **2.** PIGS ALWAYS GET SLAUGHTERED
3. BEAR IN THE CHINA SHOP **4.** BOOST FOR JOBLESS
5. JOKES IN CABLE CAR TRAP

A.

Plans to cut the dole queue were announced in the Commons last night by Employment secretary Albert Booth. He said the government subsidy given to small firms which take on extra workers in job black spots is to be extended to cover the whole country.

B.

Whenever he wants to gamble on a few hot stock tips, Mikhail Gorbachev can go to the source. Last week, when he visited the seat of American capitalism, employees of the New York Stock Exchange [...] gave him a gold-plated member badge. As he was feted in the boardroom, Gorby told members, "I'd like very much for you to establish good links with the Russian exchanges. I'll always remember there are bulls as well as bears," he added, "because we know a lot about bears."

C.

As you no doubt have heard, China is the world's biggest emerging market: 1.2 billion potential consumers for cars, TV sets ... all the stuff we've already got. ... Chinese companies maintain a close relationship with the state enterprises from which they came and sometimes can be pressured into making loans and even donations to their old cronies. I'm also told that the Chinese consider it very impolite to turn down a request for financial assistance.

D.

Singapore: A floating oil rig struck two cable cars over Singapore harbour on Saturday, throwing seven tourists to their deaths and trapping 13 others in cars swinging 100 feet above the water ... The 13 survivors told jokes to keep from panicking as they waited all night to be rescued ...

E.

Wall Street is a thoroughfare with a river at one end and a cemetery at the other. ... Today they are at the other end of the street, dressed in black, standing at the grave, wondering who will be the next to go ... And there was the unwritten law: Bulls Can Make Money. Bears Can Make Money. Pigs Always Get Slaughtered. ...
After all, the Drexel affair is only the latest float in a parade of American infamies. They date back to the early 19th century, when a hustler named Daniel Drew delivered some livestock to the plutocrats Henry and John Jay Astor. On the last three days of the trip from Ohio to New York, Drew refused to let his cattle drink. Just before they clomped up to the weighing station, he let the animals slake their thirst at a shallow creek. Appraising the swollen cattle as they weighed in, Henry Astor was proud to have bought "a fine herd". The next morning he looked out over a group of scrawny, dehydrated creatures. "I have been sold watered stock!" he bellowed, and Wall Street gained a new term for swindle.

B, C, E: Time Magazine, 25 May 1992, 28 November 1994, 26 February 1995

Ⓥ Word aid

application	Bewerbung
bear	Baissier
broker	Makler
bull	Haussier
cable car	Gondelbahn
crony	Kumpan
dole queue	Schlange vor dem Arbeitsamt
extend	verlängern
fete	feiern
gamble	spekulieren
loan	Kredit
oil rig	Bohrinsel
request	Bitte, Forderung
slake one's thirst	seinen Durst löschen
stock exchange	Börse
subsidy	Subvention
thoroughfare	Durchgangsstraße

2 Chapter

Euromania

✻ **OUR STORY: Beer or not beer – that is the question**

! **THE ARTICLE: The Euro-Tree**

Whet your appetite

Some European commissions seem to have a good sense of humour. And a lot of time. Carrots, they say , are no longer vegetable but fruit, and cucumbers have to be curved. Is it really of importance how bushy a Christmas tree is or what the diameter of an apple should be? Having a European Union appears to mean standardising everything from salaries to wine bottles.

Time for a smile

Marketing in Brussels:

What would happen if the experts of the European Union bought the Sahara?

Well, the sand in the Sahara would double within a year.

Marketing in Moscow:

What would happen if the Sahara belonged to Russia?

Within three months there wouldn't be any sand left.

(*) Beer or not beer – that is the question

Tony Strange (T), Mick Disney (M) in an Irish pub in Germany

M: Well, there's no beer like a real Guinness.

T: Well, that's it really. But did you know that according to German norms it's not a beer at all?

M: What do you mean: not a beer? What do you think it is? Chocolate?

T: Well, I'll have to come back to that one later because chocolate's got a problem with its identity as well. And so has Guinness. It's not permitted to call it 'beer'. It doesn't meet the specifications.

M: What the hell should we call it? Water?

T: You can call it Guinness, but not beer. Here in Germany a beer has to meet the criteria of the German purity rules.

M: German purity rules? I read somewhere that the pipes were full of bacteria anyway.

T: You may well be right. But as a former lawyer I have to refer you to the rules.

M: What was it you said about chocolate?

T: Well, the European Commission decreed to call it vegelate because it had more vegetable oil in it then cocoa butter, or something like that. English chocolate doesn't meet the EC-norm.

M: What does it matter what you call it, as long as it tastes good.

T: Mick, you're a simple fellow. It's a question of quality.

M: It's all a stupid waste of money if you ask me.

T: There are other wastes of money, too. For example, the whole Euro-standards. Lakes of wine and mountains of butter.

M: And I heard a joke that German Euro-MPs wanted to grade cheese in a certain way.

T: That wasn't a joke. It was true. The milk should all be pasteurised. The result is hard yellow cheeses like those boring German ones.

M: I bet the Italians and French liked that.

T: Yeah, if I remember well, the Italians then made some of their own rules so that the German noodles didn't qualify. And by the way there's a rumour going round that they want to standardise the size of your bits and pieces if you want to call yourself a man.

M: Ughh! I'm sure it'll come to that. And what about women? Waitress, or waiter or 'wait-it' or whatever, another Guinness, please. I think I'll call it Black Irish Gold from now on.

Word watch

Task 1: Scanning for keywords

Find the three words in the text that have almost the same meaning as *norms*.

c _ _ _ _ _ _ _
s _ _ _ _ _ _ _ _ s
s _ _ _ _ _ _ _ _ _ _ _ _ s

Task 2: In other words

Do you remember what they said in the dialogue?

Guinness doesn't *fulfil* the specifications.	Guinness doesn't .... the specifications.
Under the German law it's not a beer.	.... German law it's not a beer.
I've to *remind* you *of* the rules.	I've to .... you ... the rules.
Euro-MPs wanted to *classify* cheese.	Euro-MPs wanted to .... cheese.
The European Commission *decided* to call it vegelate.	The European Commission .... to call it vegelate.
I have to refer you to the *regulations*.	I have to refer you to the ....

Task 3: Complete the business idiom: One verb – five phrases

---- {
- the terms of a contract
- the delivery deadline
- the customer needs
- the EC-norm
- precise specifications

P Word power

Task 4: Wordfinder's corner

noun	verb	adjective	noun
specification	....	long	....
standard	....	wide	....
classification	....	high	....
qualification	....	bushy	....

Task 5: Guesswork

Read the following article without looking at the wordlist. Then come back and guess what the words in *italics* mean.

1. *Lo,* unto us a Eurotree is born.
   A. Love B. Look C. Lose
2. It has been decreed that *henceforth* all Christmas trees shall be standardised.
   A. in future B. by force C. at last
3. Symmetry will be *attained* by proper branch formation.
   A. achieved B. checked C. qualified
4. Neither should cuts to branches be *evident.*
   A. credible B. visible C. admissible
5. ... and there shall be no *lichen* or *moss* on the *bark.*
   A. Locher / Mistel / Borke
   B. Zapfen / Äste / Stamm
   C. Flechte / Moos / Rinde
6. They will be *legislating* what size snowflake we should have next.
   A. make a law B. make a rule C. decree

❗ The Euro-Tree

It has been decreed that henceforth all Community Christmas trees shall be standardised according to strict EC criteria.

Lo, unto us a Euro-Tree is born. Henceforth, the British yule tree shall, if it wishes to be classified, meet precise specifications on bushiness, length, width, stem, colour, freshness, symmetry and regularity of needles.

The Christmas Tree Growers' Association of Western Europe, under its venerable director, Major General Tony Richardson, has moved to harmonise the fruits of the forest into 'first quality', 'second quality' and 'unclassified'. The aim, says General Richardson, is to produce a harmony of classification that will enable tree buyers all over Europe to know exactly what they are getting for their Ecus.

To achieve 'first quality' standard, 'the width of the tree should not be greater than the height of the tree, nor less than half the height of the tree'. However, '... if the width of the tree is greater than 1.3 times the height of the tree, the tree must be graded as unclassified'.

Degrees of symmetry will be attained by proper branch formation spiralling around the stem. Needles, says the General, must be regular, developed and well spaced. The tree must not show damage and there shall be no lichen or moss on the bark. Neither should cuts to branches be evident.

To achieve prized 'first quality' status, a tree must meet all these criteria but can be allowed one 'fault'. Two 'faults' and it becomes 'second quality'.

All clear? Perhaps it will be more so to the officials of the European Normalisation Committee (CEN), to which General Richardson will take his association's standards next year in an attempt to have them adopted as a legal EC Christmas tree norm.

'They will be legislating what size snowflake we should have next,' said a shop assistant in central London.

John McGhie, The Observer, 13 December 1992, adapted

Time for a smile

An economist is a guy who would throw you a boomerang for your birthday.
Milton Berle

Digesting the article

In **Boost your reading skills 4** on page 39 we showed you where to look for the central ideas of an article. You might be able to grasp it in less than a minute. Here is a little help from our side.

Task 6: Getting the gist

The article is about the
_ _ _ _ _ _ _ to have strict
_ _ _ _ on Christmas trees
_ _ _ _ _ _ _ by the CEN.

Task 7: Scanning for the author's standpoint

Scan the text (see **Boost your reading skills 3** on page 38) to find the passage where the author states his attitude most clearly.

Word aid

according to norms	gemäß, nach den Normen
achieve	erlangen, schaffen, leisten
admissible	zulässig
attain	erreichen, erlangen, erzielen
attempt	Versuch, Bemühung
attitude	Haltung, Einstellung
bark	Rinde
bet	wetten
bits and pieces	hier: Geschlechtsteile
boring	langweilig
born	geboren
branch	Zweig
classify	klassifizieren
cover something	hier: berichten über
criterion (plural: criteria)	Kriterium
deadline	letzter Termin
decree	verfügen, verordnen
digest	verdauen, verarbeiten
enable	ermöglichen

evident	augenscheinlich, ersichtlich
fault	Defekt, Fehler
gist	Kern, Wesentliches
grade cheese	Käse einstufen, klassifizieren
guy	Bursche, Kerl
height	Höhe
henceforth	von nun an, künftig
legislate	per Gesetz regeln
lichen	Flechte
meet a norm	einer Norm entsprechen
moss	Moos
move to	beantragen
needle	Nadel
needs	Bedürfnisse
obvious	offensichtlich
pipe	Leitung
purity rules	Reinheitsgebote (für Bier)
qualify	sich eignen, qualifizieren
refer someone to	jemanden hinweisen auf
rule	anordnen, entscheiden
seven-course meal	Menü mit sieben Gängen
size	Größe
snowflake	Schneeflocke
spaced, well ~	gut verteilt
specifications	technische Beschreibung
standardise	normieren, vereinheitlichen
stem	Stamm
waste of money	Geldverschwendung
width	Weite
yule tree	Weihnachtsbaum

Time for a smile

The new reporter was sent out by the editor to cover the story of a man who could sing opera without interruption while he was eating a seven-course meal. The reporter came back and did not write up the story.
The editor wanted to know the details. "Oh, there was not much to it. The guy had two heads."

✔ Boost your reading skills 2: Skim to get an overview

When on holiday you'll have enough time to read newspapers or magazines from cover to cover. Even then you'll *skip* articles that do not interest you. The rest of the year you cannot spend hours reading your newspaper, so it is most important to have a time-saving method. *Skimming* is a reading skill that helps you to get a quick overview of the *entire* newspaper.

What is skimming? We skim, for example, when we look through a book in a bookshop before deciding *whether* to buy it or not. We also skim when reading a newspaper. Most of us do not read all the pages in detail. We first look through the paper quickly to get an idea of the day's news before *selecting* those articles we want to read.

We have no problems doing this in our native language. It is not so easy in another language, because most of the reading we have done in a foreign language has *consisted of* the slow and careful reading of short passages. Skimming English newspapers is difficult, because journalists use a special language for *headlines*.

1. Before you start, decide what your *main* interests are.
2. Select the articles that you wish to read more *thoroughly*.
3. Mark any articles of particular interest.
4. Note down where the articles are continued. This saves a lot of page turning and fumbling.
5. Cut out any articles that might be of *lasting* interest to you.

überspringen
Überfliegen
ganz(e)
ob
auswählen
bestehen aus
Überschriften
Haupt-
gründlich
bleibend, dauernd

Your first reading task:

Skim through this book to see if there is any article that has to do with your job.

When jokes backfire

OUR STORY: It's no joking matter
THE ARTICLE: When humour is no joke

Whet your appetite

One man's meat is another man's poison. What's funny for one group of people may not be funny for another. It's often said that some nations have no humour. That's not true. Their sense of humour is just different. We must remember this before cracking jokes with business partners from abroad.

Time for a smile

The man who doesn't laugh at a funny joke is probably not employed by the man who told it.

The man who says his wife can't take a joke forgets himself.

Everything is funny as long as it happens to somebody else.
Will Rogers

My way of joking is to tell the truth.
G.B. Shaw in 'John Bull's other Island'

(*) It's no joking matter

René B. (**B**) and Robert K. (**K**) discussing humour at an Italian restaurant in Heidelberg, centre of the world.

B: (*fade in*) ... so I guess there must be a great difference between the sense of humour in different countries. Look at your comedies on TV. Actually you haven't got any.

K: What's the "Kanal fatal" if it's not a comedy?

B: Well, it's some sort of satire, but it's not funny. You know exactly what's going to happen in advance.

K: It doesn't matter. It's well acted. It cracks me up.

B: Humour's not a question of acting, Robert. It's got to do with a surprise, with ambiguity, a twist in the tail, or the joke falls flat.

K: We know you English have a very odd sense of humour. For example, who wants to laugh about a fully grown man running around wearing a woman's bra under his pullover as Benny Hill does?

B: I agree with you there. It's embarrassing.

K: In my opinion there's a lot of that cheap sex in English humour. Sex is inherent in nearly all your jokes. And it's not appropriate. Such jokes can cause offence.

B: Okay, we have sex jokes, Jewish jokes, mother-in-law jokes, ethnic jokes. What sort do you have?

K: Certainly the most popular are Kohl-jokes. Did I tell you the one about Dr. Kohl's bad English?

B: Yes, you did and I don't want to hear it again. A joke isn't amusing when you've encountered it before. And that's another thing. Here in Germany people tell the same jokes over and over and the audience laughs even though they know what's coming. Can you explain that?

K: You're hopeless, René. Stop teasing me! Cultures are simply different. And in our business dealing with international managers we have to be careful how we use humour. Especially on the international stage.

B: Right. Particulary in some cultures saving face is important. In Japan cracking jokes can be a weapon that backfires. But we're getting very philosophical, Robert. I guess I'd better shut you up with a bottle of your favourite of wine. I hope you'll see the joke when you pay the bill.

Word watch

Task 1: Scanning for keywords

Find the words that fit the definition.

make someone feel uncomfortable	*e . . . . s*
correct or suitable for a situation	*a . . . . e*
be an inseparable part or quality	*i . . . . . . t*
an instrument to fight with	*w . . . . n*
a group of listeners	*a . . . . . . e*

Task 2: In other words

Do you remember what they said in the dialogue?

A joke that *is not funny*.	A joke that ....
A good joke *makes me laugh*.	A good joke ....
Sex is *part of* all your jokes.	Sex is .... in all your jokes.
Such jokes can *hurt feelings*.	Such jokes can ....
Jokes can be a *two-edged sword*.	Jokes can be a .... that back-fires.
Stop *pulling my leg*!	Stop .... me!

Task 3: Complete the business idioms: One verb – five phrases

verb	plus phrase	meaning
	face	not to be embarrassed
	the day	solve the problem
---- {	the situation	find a solution
	someone trouble	do someone a service
	up for retirement	put aside money for later

P Word power

Task 4: Wordfinder's corner

verb	noun	verb	noun
assume	....	die	....
believe	....	embarrass	....

Task 5: Do you know the German "Fremdwort"?

English	German	English	German
inherent	....	equivalent	....
misplaced	....	routinely	....
determine	....	adequately	....

Task 6: Guesswork

First read the article on page 35 and then guess what the words in *italics* mean.
Often a hard word that you don't understand at once is explained by a second word – sometimes in the same sentence. This second word has either roughly the same or the opposite meaning.

influence ≈ persuade	belief ≈ assumption
smile ≈ flicker	direct ≠ concealed
laugh ≈ crack up	save face ≠ feel uncomfortable

1. ... managers use humour to get things done; to influence and *persuade* ...

A. überreden **B.** beraten **C.** kritisieren

2. But, when it comes to international *encounters*, it can be something of a two-edged sword.

A. incursions **B.** meetings **C.** conflicts

3. There wasn't a smile or a *flicker* except from three of my colleagues, who *cracked up* completely

A. Zucken **B.** Stirnrunzeln **C.** Lachen
A. be shocked **B.** be ashamed **C.** laugh a lot

4. In Germany, humour with *its inherent ambiguity* is likely to be *restrained*.

A. seinem typischen Ernst
B. ihm eigenen Mehrdeutigkeit
C. seiner inneren Ambivalenz

A. zurückhaltend
B. geschmackvoll
C. zügellos

5. Different cultures have different beliefs and *assumptions* which can determine when humour is considered *appropriate*.

A. Ideologie **B.** Vorurteil **C.** Auffassung
A. misplaced **B.** suitable **C.** optimal

6. Communication should be direct and not *concealed*.

A. concise **B.** convinced **C.** obscure

Time for a smile

The Archbishop of Canterbury was making his first visit to New York. His advisers suggested that he should be very diplomatic and tactful in answering questions from press reporters so as to avoid any controversy. There was a huge crowd of reporters waiting to greet him and, as he stepped from the plane, one of them thrust a microphone in his face and said: "Say, Bishop, what's your opinion of the large number of brothels in Manhattan?"
Remembering that he had to be tactful, the Archbishop said cautiously: "Are there any brothels in Manhattan?"
The following morning the headlines of the New York Times read: ARCHBISHOP'S FIRST QUESTION ON ARRIVING IN NEW YORK – "ARE THERE ANY BROTHELS IN MANHATTAN?"

When humour is no joke

On the international stage, jokes can be something of a two-edged sword, Jean-Louis Barsoux reports.

All over the world, managers use humour to get things done, to influence and persuade, to motivate and unite, to say the unspeakable and to aid change. It is one of the least understood but most powerful weapons in the manager's armoury. But, when it comes to international encounters, it can be something of a two-edged sword.

Sir Brian Wolfson, the much-travelled chairman of British Leisure Group Wembley plc, offers an example: 'A couple of years ago, a few of us were speaking at an international management conference in Portugal with simultaneous translation. I decided to be funny and died an absolute death. There wasn't a smile or a flicker except from three of my colleagues, who cracked up completely, not at the jokes, but at the effect they were not having on the audience.'

But worse than the mild embarrassment or frustration of a joke simply falling flat is the possibility of causing offence or confusion through the misplaced use of humour. Different cultures have different beliefs and assumptions which can determine when humour is considered appropriate.

For example, in cultures where the desire to avoid uncertainty is high, as in Germany, humour with its inherent ambiguity is likely to be restrained. Levity will be welcomed to the extent that it contributes to the working environment and supports the high task-orientation which characterises many German companies. But German managers are less likely to use humour tactically, as a means of deflecting criticism or challenging authority. Communication should be direct and not concealed.

Status is another important consideration. In more hierarchical cultures, such as France, seniority is largely determined by intellectual achievement, in the form of academic credentials. It follows that French cadres are keen to avoid being branded as lightweight.

Similarly, in cultures where saving face is important, the use of humour will also be more regulated. For example, in many Western business cultures, teasing is routinely used as a means of social control.

However, in certain Asian cultures, 'making fun of someone' may not adequately save face, and may leave managers feeling uncomfortable. In Japan, for instance, managers use after-hours drinking as their functional equivalent of criticising with humour, because what is said when drunk does not count the following day thus saving face [...]

Jean-Louis Barsoux, The Times, 26 January 1995

Digesting the article

Task 7: Did you get the message?

Are these statements true (T) or false (F)?

1. Jean-Louis Barsoux suggests that jokes should be avoided on the international stage. ☐☐
2. The worst that can happen is when a joke falls flat. ☐☐
3. In Western business cultures managers often use humour when they give instructions to their employees. ☐☐
4. Japanese managers avoid using humour as a means of criticising in formal situations. ☐☐

Task 8: Getting the gist

(see **Boost your reading skills** 4, page 39)

Thesis: Humour is a .... However, managers often do .... on the international stage.

Warning: Jokes that are .... country can .... in .... country.

Examples: Germany: jokes are .... rather than in serious discussions.

France: jokes should not be used .... - ....

Asia: jokes can easily make your partners ....

Ⓥ Word aid

adequate	angemessen
adviser	Berater
ambiguity	Mehrdeutigkeit, Doppelsinn
armoury	Waffenarsenal
assume	annehmen, vermuten
avoid	vermeiden
backfire	ins Auge gehen
bra	Büstenhalter
brothel	Bordell
cause offence	Anstoß erregen, beleidigen
cautiously	vorsichtig, behutsam
conceal	verbergen, verschleiern
concise	kurz, knapp
contribute	beitragen
crack up	sich vor Lachen kugeln
deflect criticism	Kritik ablenken
encounter	Begegnung, Treffen
extent	Maß, Ausmaß
fall flat, a joke falls flat	ein Witz kommt nicht an
flicker	Zucken (um die Mundwinkel)
incursion	Einfall, Eindringen
inherent	innewohnend, eigen
levity	Frivolität
nutshell	Nußschale
odd	sonderbar
persuade	überreden
restrained	zurückhaltend, maßvoll
retirement	Pensionierung, Ruhestand
save face	das Gesicht wahren
suitable	angemessen
support	unterstützen
take a joke	über einen Witz lachen können
tease	hänseln
thrust	stoßen, schieben, stecken
two-edged	zweischneidig
uncertainty	Ungewißheit
one man's meat is another man's poison	des einen Leid, des andern Freud

✔ Boost your reading skills 3: Scan to get an answer to a question

Scanning is the reading skill we use when we want to find the answer to a specific question. We use it when we consult the *Yellow Pages* to find the nearest Chinese restaurant, or when we look up a name in an encyclopaedia.

Branchenverzeichnis

We also use it when reading a newspaper to find out what is going on in Wall Street or the results of an *election*. At this stage we are not *concerned* with understanding the whole article or text but only with *locating* one piece of information.

Wahl; hier: interessiert
auffinden

1. Skim the newspaper before you scan and get an overview of the lay-out of the material you are scanning. This *enables* you to save the time that many people spend hunting around in the wrong sections for the information they *desire*.
   ermöglichen
   wünschen
2. Once you have found the *relevant* part of the passage, read more slowly and more carefully until you find the specific piece of information *required*.
   betreffend
   benötigen
3. Concentrate on what you are looking for. If you look for the name of a town, you will need to look for *initial capital letters*. If it is figures, ignore all the words. If you scan for facts stop at *key words relevant* to the information you are looking for.
   große Anfangsbuchstaben
   Schlüsselwort; wichtig
4. Run your eyes vertically down the *columns* of the article as fast as you can. Do not get *distracted* at this stage by ideas or information you might otherwise be interested in at another time.
   Spalte
   ablenken
5. Stop and note down the answer. Do not continue reading the passage at this *stage*.
   Stufe
6. Your notes are the *skeleton* on which the meat of the material can be placed later.
   Skelett

✔ Boost your reading skills 4: Grasping the central idea

While skimming and scanning are both *superficial* kinds of reading, reading for the main ideas *demands* more of our attention. We need to understand more fully what the writer is trying to *convey.* We are not *concerned with* all the details of the passage and we do not have to read slowly in order to arrive at the *main ideas.*

oberflächlich; erfordern; mitteilen; interessiert an; Hauptgedanken

Try to read *slightly* faster than you normally do, not so fast that you completely *lose* the *sense* of what you are reading, but not slowly enough to *take in* all the minor details.

ein wenig; verlieren; Sinn; aufnehmen

Do not *waste* time on trying to remember dates, figures and names. You are just looking for the main thoughts and *conclusions*. By the way, in newspapers the first and the last paragraphs are the most important ones. It helps to know the structure of three *frequent* types.

verschwenden; Schlußfolgerung; häufig

***Explanatory* paragraphs** *erläuternd*

They *commence* with a statement about what is to be explained, which is followed by a series of steps to a conclusion. Concentrate on the first sentences and on the last sentences, which *contain* the conclusion. The middle of the paragraph will contain the *less* important details.

beginnen; enthalten; weniger

***Descriptive* paragraphs** *beschreibend*

They contain an *expansion* of ideas on a subject that has been introduced *previously.* They are often not so important as those that introduce main elements.

Erweiterung; vorher

***Linking* paragraphs** *verbindend*

They join other paragraphs and contain key information. They *summarise* the contents of what has *preceded* and what follows. Linking paragraphs can be very useful as a *guide.*

zusammenfassen; vorangehen; Führer

Supermarkets the American way

OUR STORY: Where the customer is not king
THE ARTICLE: American chain buys German supermarket

Whet your appetite

Part of a country's culture can be experienced in shops. We are talking about service culture. Some nationalities do not have a good feeling for service. They regard serving people as a lowly task. Our article deals with an American take-over and the change in service culture.
And what about your experiences? Have you been served badly in the last few weeks?

Time for a smile: How to get better service

A man walked up to the desk of a hotel and asked for a room.
"Have you a reservation?" asked the indifferent clerk.
"No. But I've been coming here every year for 12 years, and I've never had to have a reservation."
"Well, there is nothing available. We are full up, and without a reservation you can't get a room."
"Suppose the President of the United States came in. You would have a room for him, wouldn't you?"
"Of course, for the President we would find a room."
"Alright,"said the man. "Now I'm telling you that the President isn't coming here tonight. So give me his room."

(*) Where the customer is not king

Emily (**E**) from England, who has lived in Germany for about two years, is shopping together with Steve (**S**) who has just arrived from the USA.

S: Wow, look at this nasty queue. Why do they only have two check-outs at this outlet?

E: Perhaps the Handelsyard doesn't have enough money to employ more people, but I don't think that's the reason.

S: It seems to me there's no service mentality. Look, there's nobody to help with bag-packing after the checkout.

E: As far as I know Handelsyard has been taken over by one of your American retailers Wal-Mart.

S: Well, it remains to be seen whether that will bring about better service. It should bring prices down though.

E: Oh, why is that?

S: These Wal-Mart stores are twice as big as a football pitch. They buy huge quantities so they can get big discounts. And they spend a lot of money training their staff to deal with customers.

E: That should certainly interest German customers. They take every opportunity to get something cheap.

S: Tell me, Emily, how does the choice here compare with back in England?

E: It's interesting that you should ask that. I've got the feeling that there's far less choice. It seems to me they only go for a limited number of brands.

S: That's what I noticed, too. There are a few staple foods but no great choice of foodstuffs from outside Germany. They cater to a very conservative taste.

E: Well, I guess that's true. I miss the spicy food from back home – a good curry for example.

S: Or a good hamburger or hot dog.

E: Oh, dear me. I don't know if I'd miss that sort of thing. By the way, where do you think that sort of fast food comes from?

S: Why, they are our American national dishes. Our staple diet.

E: It's all German cuisine. Frankfurter from, guess where! Hamburger from, well, where do you think?

S: Oh, my God!

Word watch

Task 1: Scanning for keywords

A. Food

the most important food of a nation	*s . . . . . f . . .*
kind of food a person eats every day	*d . . .*
type of food, also a plate	*d . . .*

B. Around the supermarket

individual store of a chain	*o . . . . .*
where you pay for your food	*c . . . .*
company that sells goods to the public	*r . . . .*
product made by a particular company	*b . . . .*
reduction in price	*d . . . .*

Task 2: In other words

Do you remember what they said in the dialogue?

Handelsyard has been *bought* by Wal-Mart.	Handelsyard has been .... by Wal-Mart.
Well, *let's wait and see* ...	Well, it ....
They *provide food for* a very conservative taste.	They .... a very conservative taste.
How does the *variety of food* here compare with back in England?	How does the .... here compare with back in England?
They only go for a limited number of *products.*	They only go for a limited number of ....

Task 3: Our business idioms: One verb – five phrases

---- {
about better service
down prices
in an expert
into service
to an end

P Word power

Task 4: Wordfinder's corner

verb	noun	verb	noun
employ	....	associate	....
choose	....	shop	....

Task 5: Guesswork

Read the following article without looking at the wordlist. Then come back and guess what the words in *italics* mean.

1. European shopkeepers had a *nasty* start to 1998.
A. dirty **B.** unpleasant **C.** difficult

2. The more knowing were further *taken aback* when the American Wal-Mart bought Germany's huge Wertkauf chain.
A. disappointed **B.** shocked **C.** surprised

3. Wal-Mart, placed 21 hypermarkets at the heart of Europe's *complacent* retail sector.
A. bankrott **B.** benachbart **C.** selbstgefällig

4. Wal-Mart threatens retailers with their *addiction* to high margins ...
A. Sucht nach **B.** Hoffnung auf **C.** Aussicht auf

5. ... an approach known in the trade as "*pile 'em high and sell 'em cheap*".
A. Teures billig
B. volle Regale und billige Waren
C. viele Filialen und billige Waren

6. Wal-Mart comes to Europe *lean, mean* and cash-rich.
A. mager, gemein
B. verschlankt, durchschnittlich
C. leise und heimlich

American chain buys German supermarket

European shopkeepers had a nasty start to 1998. After a tough autumn and a disappointing Christmas the more knowing were further taken aback when the American retail giant, Wal-Mart, bought Germany's huge Wertkauf chain on New Year's Eve, giving it 21 hypermarkets across the country and placing it at the heart of Europe's complacent retail sector.

Wal-Mart threatens European retailers, with their addiction to high margins, by taking to the extreme an approach known in the trade as "pile 'em high and sell 'em cheap". Whether this approach will work in Europe remains to be seen.

American Wal-Mart stores are typically twice the size of a football pitch (four times the size of a typical European supermarket) and all are stacked with branded quality goods priced to move with deep discounts. Wal-Mart invests heavily in staff training; its employees greet shoppers personally and pack their bags for them at the check-out, offering a level of service normally associated in Europe only with stores that cater to the wealthy.

This philosophy has made Wal-Mart the world's largest retailer. The company operates 3,300 Wal-Marts, Sam's Clubs (membership-only warehouse stores) and Wal-Mart Supercentres in America, Argentina, Canada and Puerto Rico and, by franchise, in Brazil, China, Indonesia and Mexico.

Wal-Mart comes to Europe lean, mean and cash-rich. After 99 consecutive quarters showing increases in earnings, the company responded vigorously to a single down quarter in 1996, further cutting costs and upgrading its US stores by converting older, smaller Wal-Mart outlets into new Supercentres. These sell groceries as well as the traditional Wal-Mart staples.

Stephen Armstrong, European, 2–8 March 1998

Time for a smile

Self control: when you go into a supermarket to buy a quart of milk – and all you buy is a quart of milk.

Digesting the article

Task 6: Did you get the message?

Are these statements true (T) or false (F)?

1. American Wal-Mart stores are twice the size of a typical European supermarket.
2. Wal-Mart advertises cheap discounts and hopes that customers will buy higher priced branded goods as well.
3. Wal-Mart offers a high level of service because they cater to the wealthy.
4. After almost 25 years of rising profits Wal-Mart sales dropped in 1996.

Task 7: Scanning for the author's standpoint

1. What is the author's attitude towards the managers of European supermarkets?
   A. He adopts a neutral attitude.
   B. He is critical of European supermarkets.
   C. He has sympathy with European supermarkets.
2. What is the author's criticism of European supermarkets?
   A. They are efficient but too small.
   B. They thought they had nothing to fear.
   C. They do not know how to respond to the threat.
3. Which adjective shows his critical attitude towards European supermarkets?
4. What does he think of the marketing strategy of European supermarkets?
   A. Profit margins are much too high.
   B. Goods are sold too cheap.
   C. They cater only for the wealthy.
5. Which noun shows his attitude towards European supermarkets?

Ⓥ Word aid

addiction	Sucht
associate with	in Verbindung bringen mit, assoziieren
attitude	Einstellung, Haltung
available	verfügbar, vorhanden
bag	Einkaufstüte
brand	Marke, Sorte, Klasse
branded goods	Markenartikel
cash-rich	finanzkräftig
cater to / for	Kundenbedürfnisse befriedigen
chain	Firmenkette
checkout	Kasse
complacent	selbstgefällig, zufrieden
convert	umstellen, verwandeln
dish	Gericht, Mahl
earnings	Ertrag, Gewinn
employ	beschäftigen, anstellen
entrance	Eingang
established	eingeführt, gegründet
football pitch	Fußballfeld
franchise	Alleinverkaufsrecht
giant	Riese, riesig
groceries	Kolonialwaren
improve trade	das Geschäft beleben
indifferent	gleichgültig
lean	mager, abgespeckt
lowly tasks	niedere Aufgaben
margin	(Gewinn-)Spanne
mean	gemein
move with the big discounts	mit hohem Rabatt gekauft werden
nasty surprise	böse Überraschung
opportunity	günstige Gelegenheit
outlet	Filiale, Laden
price	Preis auszeichnen, Preis festsetzen

quart of milk	ca. ein Liter Milch
quarter	Vierteljahr
queue	Warteschlange
remain, it ~s to be seen	es bleibt abzuwarten
retail company	Weiterverkäufer, Einzelhändler
retailer	Weiterverkäufer, Einzelhändler
seek	hier: versuchen, sich bemühen
size	Größe, Umfang
stack	Stapel, voll-, aufstapeln
staff	Personal
staple diet	Grundernährung
staple foods	Grundnahrungsmittel
store	Laden, Geschäft
taken aback	verblüfft, bestürzt
taste	Geschmack
threaten	(be-)drohen
tough, a ~ autumn	ein harter Herbst
upgrade	aufwerten, verbessern
wealthy	wohlhabend

Time for a smile

In the High Street there were three shops, all in the same line of business and standing next to one another. Seeking to improve trade, the one on the left put up a notice: 'OLD ESTABLISHED – only goods of quality.'
The one on the right countered with: 'NEWLY ESTABLISHED – no old goods sold.'
The middle shop merely erected a sign stating: 'MAIN ENTRANCE HERE.'

Prince joins battle for language

OUR STORY: English as it's really 'spoke'

THE ARTICLE: Prince says Americans are ruining the language

A few years ago people were interested in learning famous old Oxford English. American was regarded in some quarters as slang. But as American economic success increased, the importance of American English rose with it. Language has become big business all over the world. There are large turnovers to be had whether in translating, teaching, computer-based training or documentation. The British are just beginning to realise what an advantage they have. That's why Prince Charles has joined the battle.

Time for a smile

You don't say "Cheers" when you drink a cup of tea in the bush; you say "Christ, the flies!"
Prince Charles

Newspaper strikes are a relief.
Princess Anne

Doctors bury mistakes. Judges hang them.
But journalists put theirs on the front page.

The freedom of the press works in a way that there is not much freedom from it.
Princess Grace of Monaco

(*) English as it's really 'spoke'

Mick Disney (**M**), René Bosewitz (**R**), Bryan Hemming (**B**), sitting in the English Pub in Hollerberg.

M: Well, it's great to be over here in Germany doing some TEFL teaching. I was getting bored with that course I was on in England.

B: Where did you do that course, Mick?

M: Nottingham.

B: Why did you choose Nottingham?

M: I just wanted to practise my golf every day. I hope I'll be able to do that here, too.

R: If you're a millionaire. The golf courses can ask what they want. There's no competition.

M: Where are you actually from, René? You've got an accent.

R: Near Nottingham. Don't you recognise the accent? It's the same as yours.

M: What do you mean? I haven't got any accent. Queen's English.

B: Well, you look a little like the Queen Mum, but you don't speak like her, Mick. If you knew anything about linguistics you'd know that.

M: My relations in the south told me I had a normal accent.

R: Give me strength! You talk just the same as me, Mick.

B: Just not so intelligently. Sorry, Mick.

M: A lot of my students are concerned that I'm not teaching them American English. Some of them have lived over there for a couple of years. They've got a good command of the vernacular.

R: It's a fact that British English is losing its share of the language market.

B: Right, I think we overestimate our popularity in some parts of the world. American business is spreading everywhere.

M: Slowly there. Surely the learners must realise it's better to pronounce English the way I do rather than John Wayne style.

B: Why do you think your way is right or even attractive? Maybe learners get access to Nottingham or the Midlands with your accent. Perhaps with an American accent you could reach the States, Australia, India. That could be a staggering number of people.

R: Yeah, Mick, you could be out of a job if you don't get an American accent.

M: Are you two threatening me? You're both from my area, too. I'd recognise your accents anywhere.
B: There you are, Mick. That was what we were trying to highlight at the beginning of our conversation, wasn't it? You really don't sound like Prince Charles, even though you think you do.
M: But I look better, don't I?
R: Not difficult, I reckon. It's your round, Mick.

W Word watch

Task 1: Scanning for keywords

Find the words that have almost the same meaning.

when we have rivals in business we are in	*c* . . . .
say or do things that cause fear	*t* . . . .
slice or part of the market	*s* . . . .
expand (into a new area)	*s* . . . . .
stress or emphasise	*h* . . . .

Task 2: In other words

Do you remember what they said in the dialogue?

They've got a good *knowledge* of the *language*.	They've got a good .... of the ....
I think we *are not as popular as we think*.	I think we .... our popularity.
American business is *expanding* everywhere.	American business is .... everywhere.
That could be an *amazing* number of people.	That could be a .... number of people.

Task 3: Complete the business idioms: One verb – five idioms

---- {
- a rumour
- one's business everywhere
- payments over two years
- a strike to other companies
- the costs over a year

Word power

Task 4: Wordfinder's corner

Read the article first. Then fill in the gaps using a word from the list below.

staggering	**backing**	**lucrative**
maintain	**growth**	**vernacular**

give one's .... to	give one's *support* to
the American	the American *English*
a .... market	a *profitable* market
a .... industry	an *expanding* industry
.... a position	*keep* a position
the figures are	the figures are *amazing*
.... the quality	*preserve* the quality

Find the noun

threaten	....
compete	....
produce	....

Task 5: Guesswork

Read the article on page 53 without looking at the wordlist. Then come back and guess what the words in *italics* mean.

1. The Prince of Wales highlighted the threat to *proper* English.
A. correct **B.** real **C.** right

2. He *launched* a campaign to preserve the language as a world leader.
A. ask for **B.** suggested **C.** started

3. He said his *concerns* were both cultural and commercial.
A. tasks **B.** worries **C.** plans

4. The English 2000 project is *intended* to protect the country's £500 million share of a global growth industry.
A. designed **B.** launched **C.** planned

5. Four-fifths of all electronic information was *stored* in English, he said.
A. written **B.** translated **C.** recorded

6. ... use the Internet to widen *access* to courses.
A. Zugang **B.** Interesse **C.** Werbung

7. It is impossible to *overestimate* the advantages the English language gives us in the world.
A. überschätzen **B.** übersehen **C.** voraussagen

8. Prince Charles *elaborated on* his view of the American influence.
A. ausarbeiten **B.** korrigieren **C.** erläutern

Time for a smile

If you can speak three languages you are trilingual.
If you can speak two languages you're bilingual.
If you can speak only one language – you're American.

The American language is in a state of flux based on the survival of the unfittest. *Cyril Conolly*

The American has no language. He has a dialect, a slang, provincialism, accent and so forth. *Rudyard Kipling*

We have really everything in common with America nowadays, except, of course, language. *Oscar Wilde*

❗ Prince says Americans are ruining the language

The Prince of Wales highlighted the threat to 'proper English' from the spread of American vernacular yesterday as he launched a campaign to preserve the language as a world leader.

He described American English as 'very corrupting' and emphasised the need to maintain the quality of language, after giving his backing to the British Council's English 2000 project. He said his concerns were both cultural and commercial.

At least 800 million people speak English worldwide, but increasing competition from America and Australia is threatening Britain's leading position in the lucrative language-teaching market. The English 2000 project is intended to protect the country's £500 million share of a global growth industry.

The Prince said: 'We must act now to ensure that English, and that to my way of thinking means English English, maintains its position as the world language well into the next century.'

Three quarters of the world's mail was written in English and four-fifths of all electronic information was stored in English, he said. 'It is impossible to overestimate the advantages the English language gives us in the world. The figures are staggering.'

Speaking after the launch, Prince Charles elaborated on his view of the American influence. 'People tend to invent all sorts of nouns and verbs, and make words that shouldn't be. I think we have to be a bit careful, otherwise the whole thing can get rather a mess.'

In the long term, the British Council fears that instantaneous translation could see English replaced as the main international language by Chinese within three generations. The countries of the Pacific Rim will be among the main targets of English 2000, which will help to develop new products and use the Internet to widen access to courses.

Other areas of increasing competition between British and American English include India, Eastern Europe and parts of Latin America. More than 30,000 Indian students now study in American colleges and universities, compared with 2,000 in Britain ...

John O'Leary, The Times, 24 March 1995

Digesting the article

Task 6: The article in a nutshell

Complete this summary with business words from the article.

The Prince of Wales .... a campaign to .... 'proper English' as a world .... He .... the threat to Britain's position in the lucrative language-teaching .... from the .... of American English. He emphasised the .... to .... the quality of language. The countries of the Pacific Rim will be among the main .... of a campaign to .... new .... and use the Internet to widen .... to English courses.

Word aid

access	Zugang, Zugriff
application	Anwendung
bury	begraben
command	Beherrschung
common, have in ~	gemeinsam haben
compared with	verglichen mit
competition	Konkurrenz, Wettbewerb
concern	Sorge
concerned, be ~	besorgt sein
corrupt	verderben
course	Kurs, Lehrgang
develop products	Produkte entwickeln
elaborate on one's view	seine Meinung näher erläutern
emphasise	betonen
ensure	sicherstellen, gewährleisten
except	außer
fear	befürchten
flux, be in a state of ~	im Fluß sein; sich verändern
get a mess	ein Durcheinander bekommen
get bored	sich langweilen
give backing	unterstützen
growth industry	Wachstumsbranche

highlight	hervorheben, betonen
include	mit einschließen
increase	zunehmen
instantaneous translation	Simultanübersetzung
intend	beabsichtigen
intended, be ~ to	sollen
invent	erfinden
launch a campaign	einen Feldzug starten
linguistics	Sprachwissenschaft
mail	Post
maintain a position	eine Stellung behaupten
Mum, the Queen Mum	die Königin Mutter
noun	Substantiv
overestimate	überschätzen
Pacific Rim	Anrainer des Pazifischen Ozeans
preserve	bewahren
protect	beschützen
reckon	glauben, meinen
recognise	erkennen
relations	Verwandte
relief	Wohltat
round	Runde
rubbish	Unsinn
share	Anteil
spread	Verbreitung
spread a rumour	ein Gerücht verbreiten
spread a strike to	einen Streik ausdehnen auf
spread one's business everywhere	sein Geschäft nach allen Seiten hin ausweiten
spread the costs over a year	Kosten auf ein Jahr verteilen
spread payments over two years	Zahlungen über ein Jahr strecken
staggering number	verblüffend große Zahl
store	speichern
survival	Überleben
target	Ziel
TEFL	Teaching English as a Foreign Language
threaten	drohen
vernacular	Umgangssprache

How to kick-start Germany's economy

OUR STORY: Sauna economics

THE ARTICLE: The radical recipe for Bonn

Whet your appetite

All is not as well in Germany as it used to be. Mr Henkel, spokesman for the leaders of German industry, is a man with visions and plans. He has some clear ideas about what is to be done to drag Germany's economy out of the mud again. Read on to find out what his opinions are on this theme.

Time for a smile

Life is what happens while you are making other plans.
John Lennon

I was warm in bed, and suddenly I'm part of a plan.
Woody Allen

Everyone takes the limits of his own vision for the limits of the world.

What is the difference between a chess player and a civil servant?
A chess player moves every now and then.

⊛ Sauna economics

Fritz von Brausewitz[1] (**B**) is discussing the economic and political situation with J. Rutert (**R**), director of technical matters at a well-known mechanical engineering company. They are in the sauna.

B: Well, J.R., it's what I've been telling you for years. The crucial thing in Germany is to become flexible. The president of your BDI, Henkel, said it very clearly indeed. And at the moment you're not. That's why you've got five million unemployed people here.

R: That's only one reason why we have so many unemployed. There are others like the famous shareholder value.

B: What's that got to do with it?

R: Well, the company has to produce as much profit as possible. That means reducing costs.

B: And one important cost is personnel. So fire them! It's very short-sighted.

R: I agree with you. But it's what our investors want. They argue it makes the company more competitive.

B: It depends on your point of view. Other people might say the companies are exploiting their employees.

R: That's an interpretation, too, I guess. What other solutions did Henkel suggest for Germany's problems?

B: Well, he said that we needed to improve standards at universities to keep the country at the forefront of technology.

R: That's certainly something that I can accept. What about tax? Was that mentioned?

B: It was the old story. Reduce tax for companies, then investors will be interested in spending more on German industry.

R: It might be the same old story but there's a lot of truth in it. But what about the normal people? Shall their tax burden be reduced?

B: Of course, because we avoid the situation that many of the people stop spending. When they have more, they spend more. And that's good for the growth of industry.

R: Well, I agree with him. But the challenge is to find a government that will carry out these tax reforms.

B: You could try England.

R: Ha ha, joke of the day from the bad joke himself.

[1] Why don't you meet Fritz, the castle-seller in *Small Talk for Big Business. Business conversation für bessere Kontakte*, rororo 60439.

Word watch

Task 1: Scanning for keywords

Replace the words in *italics* with the words used in the dialogue.

The *important* thing is to become flexible.	c . . . . . .
They argue it makes the company more *efficient*.	c . . . .
We need to improve *efficiency* at universities.	s . . . .
Shall their tax *load* be reduced?	b . . . . .
And that's good for the *expansion* of industry.	g . . . . .

Task 2: In other words

Do you remember the way it was said in the dialogue?

There are other reasons like the famous *stock exchange rate.*	There are other reasons like the famous ....
What other solutions did he *propose* for Germany's problems?	What other solutions did he .... for Germany's problems?
But the *task* is to find a government that will carry out these tax reforms.	But the .... is to find a government that will carry out these tax reforms.

Task 3: Complete the business idioms: One verb – five idioms

---- {
out tax reforms
forward a debt
on business through ads
aims through to the end
away with enthusiasm

Time for a smile

It's easy to be a humorist when you have the whole government working for you. *Will Rogers*

Word power

Task 4: Wordfinder's corner

Read the article on page 61 before you do these exercises.

Find a word that means the opposite

secure (adj.) jobs	.... jobs
increase costs	.... costs
avoid reforms	.... reforms

Find a word that has a similar meaning

propose reforms	.... reforms
keep a position	.... a position
raise standards	.... standards
lower tax burdens	.... tax burdens
create growth	.... growth

Find four words that have the same root as

compete {
....
....
....
....

Food for thought

The public be damned! I'm working for my stockholders.
William Henry Vanderbilt

Never invest your money in anything that eats or needs repairing.
Billy Rose

All costs walk on two legs.

Too bad that all the people who know how to run the country are busy driving taxicabs and cutting hair. *George Burns*

Task 5: Guesswork

Read the article which follows. Guess the meaning of the words in *italics*.

1. The BDI suggested an extensive plan to *kick-start* the labour marke to generate dynamic new growth in the *medium term.*

   A. rationalisieren **A.** mittelfristig
   B. entlasten **B.** auf Dauer
   C. ankurbeln **C.** Mittelstand

2. In eight areas we suggested concrete steps to improve the *manufacturing base.*

   A. working class **B.** production environment **C.** productivity

3. Germany is a country of high *environmental standards.*

   A. laws for the protection of nature
   B. norms for the purity of drinks and food
   C. regulations for the building of houses and roads

4. Germany can maintain its position only by *exploiting* to the full its potential in research and technology.

   A. ausbeuten **B.** erforschen **C.** ausnutzen

Task 6: Choose a word that fills the gap

1. These steps are crucial if Germany is to improve its ....

   A. competition **B.** competitiveness **C.** competitors

2. Enterprises need to develop the ability to be more ....

   A. modern **B.** progressive **C.** innovative

3. New .... in the global market need to be explored.

   A. opportunities **B.** chances **C.** prospectives

The radical recipe for Bonn

Germany cannot *avoid* implementing lasting reforms. Only when the conditions for investment are right can enterprises create profitable jobs. Why are too few jobs being created? Because businesses are burdened with excessively high costs and taxes.

At the beginning of 1997 the Bundesverband der Deutschen Industrie (BDI) suggested an extensive plan to kick-start the labour market and generate dynamic new growth in the medium term. In eight areas, we suggested concrete steps to improve the manufacturing base. These steps are crucial if Germany is to improve its competitiveness and secure and create jobs.

1. Flexibility

Enterprises need to develop the ability to be more innovative. The rapid change of the global market leaves no time to rest. To secure and extend international competitiveness remains a daily challenge. Not only do quality standards need to be at an international level but also new opportunities in the dynamic global market need to be explored more efficiently. Much needs to be improved in the areas of service and customer relations.

2. Qualifications

We need to improve qualifications at schools and universities. Germany is a country of high costs, high environmental and social standards and high income demands. Germany can maintain its position among international competitors only by exploiting to the full its potential in research and technology.

3. Tax

It is absolutely essential to lower the tax burden on German businesses to a level that bears comparison with other countries. Standort Deutschland needs to become more attractive to national and foreign investors. Germany needs a tax reform agreement that creates jobs and encourages domestic and foreign investment.

Tax reform is also good for the state, because it leads to more growth, more jobs and higher tax income. Tax burdens play an important role in the competition for global mobile investment capital. Examples are countries such as Britain, Austria and Sweden which have bravely cut tax burdens for business.

The European, 23 – 29 March 1998, abbridged

Digesting the article

Task 7: Complete the key phrases

1. Lasting reforms must be ....
2. New opportunities need to be ....
3. Research and technology must be ....
4. Service and customer relations have to be ....
5. The tax burden on German businesses has to be ....
6. Qualifications at schools and universities must be ....

Word aid

argue	argumentieren, streiten
avoid	vermeiden, herumkommen um
bear comparison with	den Vergleich erlauben mit
burden	belasten
carry aims through to the end	Ziele bis zum Ende verfolgen
carry away with enthusiasm	begeistern
carry forward a debt	eine Schuld fortschreiben
carry on business	Geschäft weiter betreiben
carry out tax reforms	Steuerreformen durchführen
challenge	Herausforderung
chess	Schach
civil servant	Beamter
competitive	konkurrenzfähig
competitiveness	Wettbewerbsfähigkeit
competitor	Konkurrent, Mitbewerber
depend on	abhängen von
efficient	rationell, leistungsfähig, tüchtig
encourage	ermutigen
enterprise	Unternehmen, Firma
environmental standards	Umweltnormen
essential	wichtig, wesentlich
exploit	ausbeuten
extend	vergrößern, erweitern
extensive plan	umfassender Plan

generate	schaffen, erzeugen
growth	Wachstum
implement reforms	Reformen durchführen
improve standards	die Qualität verbessern
income demands	Gehaltsforderungen
kick-start	anschieben, ankurbeln
labour market	Arbeitsmarkt
maintain one's position	seine Stellung behaupten
manufacturing base	Produktionsstandort
medium term, in the ~ ~	mittelfristig
needs	Bedürfnisse
opportunity	Chance, Gelegenheit
rapid change	schneller Wandel
reduce costs	Kosten senken
remain	bleiben
research	Forschung
secure jobs	Arbeitsplätze sichern
service warranty	Wartungsvertrag
shareholder value	Kurswert der Aktien
suggest	vorschlagen, anregen
tax burden	Steuerlast
unemployed	arbeitslos

Time for a smile: The Dilbert Principle

If there's no market for your product, sometimes you can create one. The most effective methods for creating a market include creating a problem and providing the solution:

PROBLEM YOU CREATE	SOLUTION YOU OFFER
Write bad software	Sell upgrades
Tell people they stink	Sell deodorant
Build unreliable products	Sell service warranties

Scott Adams

Destress in salt water

OUR STORY: Float your weight away

THE ARTICLE: Destressed executives in retreat from strain

Whet your appetite

"An executive is a fat ulcer with authority" as the saying goes. Well, it's the old question why some stressed executives tend to get fat under stress while others dwindle away. What can be done? Our article has the answer: float your stress away in a bath tub of salty water.

Time for a smile

I like long walks, especially when they are taken by people who annoy me. *Fred Allen*

Go jogging? What, and get hit by a meteor? *Robert Benchley*

God heals, the doctor takes the fee. *Benjamin Franklin*

(*) Float your weight away

Tony (**T**), a trainer from Pelc Com.be.nations in Heidelberg, is talking to James Kelly (**J**), a young would-be executive from Hollerberg Printing Presses. Tony, although only one metre fifty, is very much into health:

J: I can't understand it. I've been putting weight on since I've been here in Germany and I'm not eating as much as I did.

T: You doing any sport?

J: Gee, I've no time for that. A future executive has to put in at least sixty hours a week.

T: Well, you should be jogging two or three times a week with a swim in between. And you should use a special formula to find your optimal heart frequency for training. Are you under a lot of pressure?

J: Yes, I am.

T: Well, if you're stressed or anxious, you build fat around your abdomen.

J: I would have thought that if I was stressed, I would lose weight, through nervousness and so on.

T: Some people do shrivel when exposed to pressure, but you're obviously not one of them.

J: Yes, at the moment my body and soul seem really out of tune.

T: Yeah, you've got to strengthen your cardiovascular system.

J: More sports. Grrhh, I ...

T: Not sport. There's another method for people susceptible to putting on fat. You've got to detox. Get rid of your poisons.

J: And just how do I do that?

T: Just fill your bath full of salt water at body temperature and float naked in it for an hour or two.

J: Salt water? Man, are you being serious or is this some more of your British black humour?

Word watch

Task 1: Scanning for keywords

Find the words in the dialogue that have almost the same meaning.

veins and arteries of the heart	*c . . . . r s . . . . m*
manager in a key position	*e . . . . e*
middle of your body	*a . . . . . n*
in harmony	*in t . . .*

Task 2: In other words

Do you remember the way it was said in the dialogue?

Are you under a lot of *stress*?	Are you under a lot of ....?
If you're stressed or anxious you build fat around your *middle.*	If you're stressed or anxious you build fat around your ....
Some people do *shrink* when *put under* pressure.	Some people do .... when .... to pressure.
Get rid of your poisons.	....
There's another method for people *with a tendency* to putting on fat.	There's another method for people .... to putting on fat.
Fill your bath full of salt water and *lie* naked in it.	Fill your bath full of salt water and .... naked in it.

Task 3: Complete the business idioms: One verb – five idioms

---- {
in sixty hours a week
the record straight
him in the picture
pressure on
on weight

P Word power

Task 4: Wordfinder's corner

Read the article on page 69 before you do these exercises.

Find a word that means the opposite

stress	....	cognitive	....
shrivel	....	increase	....

Find a word that has a similar meaning

mind	....	belly	....
relax	....	rise	....
illness	....	stress	....
answer	....	out of tune	out of ....

Find the noun

execute	....
respond	....
float	....
relax	....
harmonise	....

Time for a smile

The only way to keep your health is to eat what you don't want, drink what you don't like and do what you'd rather not. *Mark Twain.*

My wife is on a diet of coconuts and bananas. She hasn't lost any weight, but can she climb a tree! *Henry Youngman*

All the things I like doing are either immoral, illegal or fattening. *Oscar Wilde*

A man is as old as the woman he feels. *Groucho Marx*

Task 5: Guesswork

Read the following article without looking at the wordlist. Come back and guess what the words in *italics* mean.

1. As the Easter weekend approaches, stressed-out executives should avoid the *temptation* of chocolate eggs ...
   A. Genuß **B.** Versuchung **C.** Suchen

2. Instead, they should use the time to *detox* and destress their bodies and minds ...
   A. entgiften **B.** entspannen **C.** stärken

3. The body's response to stress is extraordinarily complex: some people *thrive on* it, while others suffer and *shrivel* under the pressure.
   A. leiden an **A.** zittern
   B. blühen auf **B.** verfallen
   C. leben auf **C.** bauen ab

4. Stress can lead to an *increase in any susceptibility* to disease.
   A. an increased resistance
   B. a strengthening of the immune system
   C. a weakening of the immune system

5. Floating naked in salty water is the closest most people will come to *sensory deprivation.*
   A. absence of stimuli
   B. stimulating of the senses
   C. deep relaxation

Destressed executives in retreat from strain

As the Easter weekend approaches, stressed-out executives should avoid the temptation of chocolate eggs and freshly baked cakes. Instead, they should use the time to detox and destress their bodies and minds so that they return to work with a positive attitude and extra energy.

The body's response to stress is extraordinarily complex: some people thrive on it, while others suffer and shrivel under the pressure. But whatever an individual's short-term response, the accumulated effect of stressful days and nights is ill health; it can even be a killer.

Stress hormones, such as hydrocortisone, may at first protect the body's defence system but overexposure can cause a cascade of negative changes. According to a recent American study, anxiety adds fat around the abdomen. Worse, it can also lead to a rise in blood pressure, a weakening of the immune system and an increase in any susceptibility to disease. Cardiovascular disease and poor cognitive and physical function can also result.

So relaxation is an important way of harmonising body and mind. But bringing them back into balance is not as easy as it sounds – sometimes the body needs a kick start to destress the system.

If the mind and body are out of sync after too many hours rushing around, flotation is an increasingly popular method of reducing stress. Floating naked in the dark and in 25 centimetres of body-temperature salty water is the closest most people will come to sensory deprivation. Experienced floaters describe it as the deepest state of relaxation, equivalent to four or five hours of deep sleep and a way to get in tune with body and mind.

Cath Blackledge, The European, 6–12 April 1998

Time for a smile

When asked how he accounted for his good health and his old age Churchill answered: "No sports ... and the fact that I cancelled my voyage on the Titanic."

Digesting the article

Task 6: Did you get the meaning?

Are these statements true (T) or false (F)?

1. Some people need stress to be successful.
2. Anxious people tend to put on weight.
3. Cardiovascular disease is a disease of the soul.
4. Stress hormones protect the body's defence system.
5. Floating in salt water is the equivalent of a good night's rest.

Word aid

abdomen	Bauch
account for something	etwas erklären
accumulate	aufstauen, ansammeln
anxiety	Angst
approach	hier: näherkommen, nahen
attitude	Einstellung, Haltung
be into health	auf Gesundheit Wert legen
belly	Bauch
cardiovascular disease	Erkrankung der Herzkranzgefäße
cognitive	geistig
defence	Verteidigung, Abwehr
defence system	Abwehrsystem
deprivation	Entzug, Mangel
destress	entspannen
detox	entgiften
disease	Krankheit
equivalent, be ~ to	entsprechen
executives	leitende Angestellte
exposure	Ausgesetztsein, Belichtung
fat	Fett
flotation	Schweben, Treiben
increase	zunehmen, Zunahme
kick-start	Anstoß, Anschub

physical	körperlich
pressure	Druck
protect	(be-)schützen
put in sixty hours a week	60 Stunden pro Woche arbeiten
put in the picture	ins Bild setzen
put pressure on someone	jemanden unter Druck setzen
put the record straight	etwas richtigstellen
reduce	verringern
relax	(sich) entspannen
relaxation	Entspannung
response	Antwort, Reaktion
retreat	Rückzug, sich zurückziehen
sensory	sensorisch, Sinnes-
sensory deprivation	Reizentzug
short-term response	kurzfristige Reaktion
shrivel	hier: verkümmern, abbauen
strain	Anspannung
susceptibility	Empfänglichkeit
sync, be out of ~	nicht im Einklang stehen
temptation	Versuchung
thrive	gedeihen, aufblühen
tune, get in ~	in Einklang kommen
ulcer	Magengeschwür
weaken	schwächen
weight, put on ~	an Gewicht zunehmen
worse	schlimmer
would-be executive	Möchtegern-Manager

Time for a smile

The art of medicine consists in amusing the patient while Nature cures the disease. *Voltaire*

My doctor gave me six months to live, but when I couldn't pay the bill he gave me six months more. *Walter Matthau*

Anyone who goes to a psychiatrist should have his head examined. *Samuel Goldwyn*

The Elk Test

OUR STORY: Fastest car on one door

THE ARTICLE: Spin control: Opel and VW in a flip-flop

Whet your appetite

A few years ago it was a craze in Germany to talk about how good German cars were. As time went by competition has become fiercer. Now there seems to be a new madness in Germany: to try to prove that German cars are not good. German car producers "elk-test" each other's cars out of the market. Foreign competitors can only smile at the sight of German cars with their wheels in the air.

Time for a smile

Sticker on Mini: 'This was a Rolls before it went through the carwash.'

How do you double the price of a Lada?
Fill up the petrol tank.

Why does a Lada have heated rear windscreens?
To keep your hands warm when you push it.

A Trabbi makes your average Skoda look like a Ferrari.

⊛ Fastest car on one door

Tom Shanahan (T) has just passed his driving test. Now he wants to abandon the tram and get a car of his own. Michael Disney (M) and Tom driving along in Mick's Rover soft top.

T: Well, it'll be great to have my own transport.

M: It's certainly time you got mobile. You waste hours legging it all over Heidelberg.

T: I'm not complaining. Walking is a remedy for losing weight. In Ireland, back home it's commonplace to walk.
(*Mick has to swerve hard to avoid hitting a cyclist.*)

M: Did you see that? Damn this system! Fancy giving a cyclist a green light at the same time as a car. And cyclists insist on going down one-way streets the wrong way. They don't have lights on their bikes.

T: Calm down, Mick. Don't smear the reputation of the Germans for trying to organise every detail on the road.

M: Trying to overorganise, you mean.

T: It'll be different when I have my Flog.

M: Flog? That might be dangerous. Have you heard of the Elk test?

T: Who hasn't? But that was the new U-Class of Mercenary Star.

M: Yeah, the fastest vehicle on one door. But now the German car producers are testing each others models. They call it competition testing.

T: I see. A sort of bench-marking?

M: More or less. And FV and Polec have also launched new models. At some point all of them were lying on their backs with their wheels in the air.

T: I guess all cars would tip or flip over when put through this sort of test.

M: Maybe. Anyway there's a boom in ESP, that's 'electronic stability programs' to keep the car upright.

T: It all sounds very complicated. Perhaps I should get a bike. Is there an Elk test for that, do you think?

Word watch

Task 1: Scanning for keywords

Find the words in the dialogue that have almost the same meaning.

very usual or normal	*c . . . . e*
dirty or blacken something	*s . . . r*
solution for putting things right	*r . . . . y*
comparison of systems of the same type	*b . . . . - . . . . . . g*

Task 2: In other words

Do you remember the way it was said in the dialogue?

The fastest vehicle on *its side.*	The fastest vehicle on ....
There's a *great demand for* ESP.	There's a .... in ESP.
FV and Polec have also *marketed* new models.	FV and Polec have also .... new models.
They call it a *bench-marking test against rival cars.*	They call it .... testing.
All cars would *topple* over when put through this sort of test.	All cars would .... or .... over when put through this sort of test.

Task 3: Complete the business idioms: One verb – five idioms

---- {
through a test
off until later
into perspective
up the money for a project
down on paper

Time for a smile

I've just bought my wife a Stradivari.
Have you? Does she like sports cars?

(P) Word power

Read the article on page 76 before you do these exercises.

Task 4: Wordfinder's corner

Find a word that has a similar meaning.

market (v)	....	competing model	....
solution	....	prestige	....
maker	....	rise rapidly	....
tip	....	control, measure	....

Task 5: Words in context

Put your solutions to *task 4* into the sentences in their correct forms.

1. A high-speed swerve is certainly something that every .... believes it must put its cars through.
2. They wanted to smear the good .... of Opel.
3. High-tech .... are emerging.
4. As Daimler saw its reputation threatened, it conducted a "bench-marking test" against .... models.

Task 6: Guesswork

Can you guess the meaning of the words in *Italics?*

1. A high-speed *swerve* is certainly something that every manufacturer believes it must *put* its car *through*.
   A. brake test **B.** crash test **C.** change of direction
   A. run through **B.** help through **C.** see through

2. Opel *brushed off* all accusations from VW.
   A. considered **B.** accepted **C.** denied

3. A sensor *gauges* a car's centre of gravity.
   A. aktiviert **B.** mißt **C.** stabilisiert

Spin control: Opel and VW in a flip-flop

"A high-speed swerve is certainly something that every manufacturer believes it must put its car through," said John Lawson, industry analyst in London at Salomon Smith Barney. "I do not believe that anyone could possibly be comfortable at launch if their car cannot pass the elk test, given the situation that Mercedes had to face."

Brushing off accusations from VW, GM's Adam Opel unit insisted Friday that it did not intend to topple the Golf IV, the latest version of the best-selling car in Europe.

A VW board member, Klaus Kocks, accused Opel of "dirty propaganda" this week, saying that it had conducted the test to smear the reputation of its rival during the Geneva auto show.

Opel admits that it ran a Golf through a series of elk tests in front of 70 Opel salesmen, who were eager to see how the new Opel Astra – a model that competes directly with the Golf – fares in the industry's hottest new safety exercise. Tests of competing cars are standard in the industry, Opel said. "The Golf went through the tests several times without any problem, but on the last time it tipped," an Opel spokesman said. "We cannot explain the hysteria from VW," said another Opel spokesman, Bruno Seifert.

Opel, however, cannot boast that it is the first to tip over a new Golf. As Daimler saw its reputation threatened last November, it conducted a "bench-marking test" against rival models. On an abandoned military airport near Stuttgart, its drivers managed to flip both an Astra and a Golf.

As images of cars with their four wheels pointed to the sky become commonplace, at least in Germany, high-tech remedies are emerging. Business has boomed for makers of computerised balancing systems that stabilise cars on tight elk-like turns.

Known as "electronic stability programs," or ESP, such sophisticated gear could eventually become as standard as airbags or anti-lock brakes, some industry officials say. Activated by a sensor that gauges a car's centre of gravity, ESP is meant to stabilise an off-balance car by gently braking its wheels or slowing the engine [...]

John Schmid, The International Herald Tribune, 7–8 March 1998

Digesting the article

Task 7: Did you get the meaning?

Are these statements true (T) or false (F)?

1. Elk tests are not absolutely necessary.
2. Opel denied testing the Golf.
3. The Golf went through the test without toppling over.
4. Computerised balancing systems are selling well.
5. All elk-tested German cars tipped and flipped.
6. Opel was the first to tip over a Golf.

Task 8: Scanning for the author's standpoint

1. What does the author think about the Elk test?

   A. Every manufacturer should run these tests.
   B. They are a typical German phenomenon.
   C. Elk tests are not realistic.

2. What's the author's opinion about the tests conducted by Opel?

   A. It was the right thing to do.
   B. Opel wanted to increase the safety of cars.
   C. They did it secretly and hoped that nobody would find out.

3. Tests of competing cars have been conducted

   A. mainly for reasons of prestige and promotion
   B. mainly for safety reasons
   C. mainly to boost the sales of ESP systems

Time for a smile: Graffiti

Ruver Cars made in the UK – absolutely safe and reliable; approved to British Standards BS 9966, (But so was the Titanic)

Ⓥ Word aid

abandoned	verlassen
abandon the tram	die Straßenbahn nicht mehr benutzen
accuse someone	jemanden beschuldigen
admit	zugeben
anti-lock brakes	ABS, nichtblockierende Bremsen
approved to British Standards	geprüfte Sicherheit, TÜV-Plakette
average	durchschnittlich
bench-mark	vergleichender Waren-, Markentest
boast	sich rühmen
brake test	Bremstest
brush off accusations	Anschuldigungen abschütteln
can	Konservendose
commonplace, become ~	alltäglich werden
compete with	im Wettbewerb liegen mit
competition testing	Vergleichstest
conduct the test	einen Test leiten, durchführen
craze	Wahnsinn
cyclist	Radfahrer
discard	wegwerfen
eager, be ~ to see	begierig sein, etwas zu sehen
elk	Elch
eventually	schließlich
fancy	man stelle sich vor
flip	umkippen, umdrehen
gauge (v)	messen
gear	Ausrüstung
hit a cyclist	einen Radfahrer anfahren
insist on	bestehen auf
launch (n)	Markteinführung
launch (v)	auf den Markt bringen
leg it all over the town	alles zu Fuß in der Stadt machen
off-balance car	ein aus dem Gleichgewicht gekommenes Auto
one-way street	Einbahnstraße

pass a test	eine Prüfung bestehen
put down on paper	zu Papier bringen
put into perspective	in Beziehung bringen, setzen
put off until later	auf später verschieben
put through a test	einem Test unterziehen
put up the money for a project	Geld für ein Projekt aufbringen
slow the engine	den Motor drosseln
smear the reputation of someone	jemandes Ruf in den Schmutz ziehen
soft top	Cabriolet
sophisticated	hochentwickelt
swerve	ausscheren
test of competition	Vergleichstest mit der Konkurrenz
threaten	bedrohen
tight turns	enge Kurven
tip (over)	umkippen
topple over	umkippen
transport, have one's own ~	sein eigenes Fahrzeug haben
turn	Kurve
waste hours	Stunden verschwenden

Time for a smile

The marvels of modern technology include the development of a soda can which, when discarded, will last forever, and a $70,000 car which, when properly cared for, will rust out in two or three years.
Paul Harwitz

9 Chapter

The price of beauty

OUR STORY: Born fat

THE ARTICLE: Fat of the land

Whet your appetite

It's not clear whether all the mass-produced pharmaceuticals are really necessary for improving people's health. Maybe companies pump them out all over the world only to improve the health of their companies. And certainly it's true of fatburners, those drugs which are supposed to eliminate our extra kilos of fat. The problem is that they might do a lot of other things, too, cause cancer, or dry out your kidneys or blow up your liver. Each one of us must decide what price beauty.

Time for a smile: Why some of us are fat

I'm amazed at people who eat a big breakfast.
How can you work up an appetite sleeping?

I think if I have a good breakfast I could go without food for the rest of the day. I think that until about lunchtime.

Most people agree that walks are good for your health.
Where I live in Beverly Hills, nobody walks. I've got one neighbour who has a little car to drive to his big car. *George Burns*

⊛ Born fat

René Bosewitz (**B**) and Robert Kleinschroth (**K**) sweating and puffing and jogging along the River Neckar and generally feeling miserable.

K: We've only done two kilometres and my archilles tendon is hurting already. My muscles and joints don't seem to perform any more.

B: I won't say you're obese, Robert, but there's too much excess fat on you for your rather weak frame.

K: What frame?

B: I mean your skeleton and tendons. They can't take it.

K: Well, what about you? You're certainly overweight with your stomach.

B: You're right. My stomach is round but with all the training we do I must say my fat has grown muscles on it. But the bottom line is that somehow my chest has dropped one metre down to my stomach. The bits and pieces have shifted a bit. That's all.

K: It's more a matter of consuming too many of the good things in life. That's why we are forced to seek the holy grail of training to keep fit.

B: By the way, did you hear that Roche are bringing out a new wonder drug, a fatburner? It really burns your fat.

K: Great idea. Let's buy a kilo first thing in the morning. For that matter let's get some shares in Roche, too. It'll take the world by storm.

B: Hey, slow down, Robert. This will be a body blow for you but it's not passed its tests yet. It is deemed to be dangerous. Maybe it causes cancer. So it's got no approval.

K: My god! What a dangerous drug. We'd better just do it our way, jogging off the pounds ...

B: And putting them all back on with your daily bottle of wine.

Word watch

Task 1: Scanning for keywords

Find the words in the dialogue that have almost the same meaning.

being very fat indeed	*o* . . . .
eat up all of something	*c* . . . . . .
a stamp which gives the okay	*a* . . . .
you buy it at the stock exchange	*s* . . . .

Task 2: In other words

Do you remember the way it was said in the dialogue?

I won't say you're *fat*, Robert.	I won't say you're ...., Robert.
There's too *big a quantity of* fat on you.	There's too .... fat on you.
This will be a *shock* for you.	This will be a .... for you.
The *final result* is that my chest has dropped one metre down to my stomach.	The .... is that my chest has dropped one metre down to my stomach.
The bits and pieces have *moved to another place*.	The bits and pieces have ....
Roche are bringing out a new wonder drug, a *fatbuster*.	Roche are bringing out a new wonder drug, a ....

Task 3: Complete the business idioms: One verb – five idioms

---- {
- the world by storm
- a body blow
- over a company
- firm action on
- risks

Ⓟ Word power

Task 4: Wordfinder's corner

Read the article on page 85 before you do these exercises.

Find a word that has a similar meaning

transpiration	....	prophecy	....
fatburner	....	put on the market	....
eat	....	estimated as being fat	....
barrier	....	last but one	....

Find the noun

approve	....	Zustimmung
exceed	....	Überschuß
compete	....	Konkurrent
obese	....	Fettleibigkeit
advise	....	Ratgeber
prescribe	....	Rezept (Arzt)

Task 5: Words in context

Put your solutions to *task 4* into the sentences in their correct forms.

1. The American drugs agency did not give its .... to the product.
2. What level of profit do you .... for next year?
3. All your .... fat must be reduced by dieting.
4. You can buy Xenical on ....
5. All your .... have patents for similar drugs, too.

Time for smile

She has been taking this anti-fat pill for three weeks. Now she's so thin that every time she walks in the park, a dog tries to bury her.

Task 6: Guesswork

Read the article. Then come back and guess the meaning of the words in *italics*.

1. The pill *shifts* fat the easy way.
   A. kills B. pushes C. reduces

2. The company *intends* to boost its bottom line.
   A. hopes B. plans C. increases

3. Earnings will be reduced by *approximately* six per cent.
   A. exactly B. more than C. round about

4. Roche was betting that Xenical would be one of its *star performers*.
   A. best sellers B. best profits C. best actors

Task 7: Scanning for facts and figures

1. Xenical might enjoy peak sales of SF ___ million a year.
2. More than ___ million people worldwide are obese.
3. Obesity: a body mass index of more than ___ kg/m^2.
4. More than ___ per cent of Americans are obese.
5. Up to ___ per cent of the adult population in Europe are estimated to be fat.
6. The market for Xenical could be worth $ ___ billion.

Time for a smile

I said to my son: "Finish up all your meat, and you'll grow and be just like Daddy." Since then he only eats vegetables. *Rodney Dangerfield*

Fat of the land

With so many overweight adults, the market could be worth $50bn.

The search for one of the holy grails of medicine – a pill that helps shift excess flesh the easy way, without patients having to work up a sweat or eat less – has taken another body blow; this time it is the turn of Swiss giant Roche to feel the pinch.

Roche's share price fell by five per cent on the news that its fatbuster pill, Xenical, had not cleared the penultimate hurdle to its launch in the gigantic and almost competitor-free American prescription market for anti-obesity drugs. Advisers to America's drugs approval agency, the Food and Drug Administration (FDA), said they could not reach a decision on whether to recommend that the pill is launched later this year because of concerns that Xenical increases the risk of developing breast cancer. Roche was betting that Xenical would be one of its star performers, enjoying peak sales of SF700 million ($470m) a year. Without the drug, it has forecast that its earnings stream will be reduced by approximately six per cent over the next five years.

It is estimated that more than 100 million people world-wide are obese – defined as having a body mass index (BMI) of more than 30 kg/m2. More than 30 per cent of Americans are obese, while Europeans are slightly slimmer, with up to 20 per cent of the adult population deemed to be officially fat.

Although an undefined proportion of obesity is believed to be of genetic origin, most is a direct result of consuming too much fat and not working hard enough to get rid of it. With so many overweight adults, the market for a prescription anti-obesity pill that has to be taken every day to keep the weight off could be worth as much as $50 billion – a tempting carrot for a drugs company hoping to boost its bottom line.

Cath Blackledge, The European, 23–29 March 1998

Digesting the article

Task 8: Scanning for the author's standpoint

1. What does the author think in general about the search for a slimming pill?
   - **A.** He thinks they have almost discovered it.
   - **B.** He thinks that doctors would not prescribe it.
   - **C.** He feels that big companies are too optimistic about it.

2. Which expressions does the author use that makes you think he is pessimistic about the future of Xenical?

3. What is the author's idea of why people get obese?
   - **A.** They consume too much and don't take enough exercise.
   - **B.** They eat too much.
   - **C.** They get fat for genetic reasons.

4. Why are the drug companies interested in producing the pill?
   - **A.** to get the edge over their competitors
   - **B.** to boost their turnover
   - **C.** to raise their company image

Word aid

adult population	Erwachsenenbevölkerung
approval	Zustimmung, Genehmigung
approximately	ungefähr
bet	wetten, setzen (auf)
body blow	Tiefschlag
body mass index	Körpergröße-Index
boost	Auftrieb geben, ankurbeln
boost the turnover	den Umsatz steigern
bottom line	Fazit
breast cancer	Brustkrebs
bury	be-, vergraben

carrot, a tempting carrot	hier: Köder
chest	Brust; Brustkorb
clear the hurdle	die Hürde nehmen
competitor-free	konkurrenzlos
concerns	Sorgen
decision, reach a ~	zu einer Entscheidung gelangen
deem	erachten
drugs approval agency	Genehmigungsbehörde für Medikamente
earnings stream	Einnahmen
estimate	schätzen
excess flesh	überflüssiges Fleisch
fatburner	Fettverbrenner
fatbuster	Fettverbrenner
fit as a fiddle	munter wie ein Fisch im Wasser
forecast	vorhersagen
frame	Körperbau
giant	Riese
holy grail	Heiliger Gral
improve	verbessern
increase a risk	ein Risiko erhöhen
joint	Gelenk
kidney	Niere
launch	Markteinführung
liver	Leber
merely	lediglich
obese	fettleibig
obesity	Fettleibigkeit
overweight	übergewichtig; Übergewicht
peak sales	Spitzenabsatz, -verkauf
penultimate hurdle	vorletzte Hürde
perform	leisten
pinch, feel the ~	knapp bei Kasse sein
prescription	Rezept (des Arztes)
prescription market	Markt für verschreibungspflichtige Medikamente
puff	schnaufen

seek the holy grail	den Heiligen Gral suchen
share price	Aktienkurs
shift	(sich) verlagern, verschieben
skeleton	Skelett
slim	schlank
star performer	Verkaufsschlager
sweat	Schweiß; schwitzen
take a body blow	einen Tiefschlag einstecken
take action	etwas unternehmen
take over a company	eine Firma übernehmen
take risks	Risiken eingehen
take the world by storm	die Welt im Sturm nehmen
tendon	Sehne
turn, it is the ~ of	die Reihe ist an
vegetable	Gemüse
weightlifting	Gewichtheben

Time for a smile

Middle age is when your age starts to show around the middle. *Bob Hope.*

You know you've reached middle age when your weightlifting consists merely of standing up. *Bob Hope*

It's hard to feel as fit as a fiddle when you're shaped like a cello.

If I'd known I was going to live so long, I'd have taken better care of myself. *Leon Eldred*

✔ Boost your reading skills 5: Guessing the meaning of unknown words

When reading this book you are *likely* to meet a number of expressions which you do not know. Do not *rush* to the nearest dictionary. First, it is not always necessary to understand every single word, and second, it is often possible to *work out* the *meaning* of a word you have never seen before. Here are a few strategies which help in the *task* of *guessing* words you do not know.

1. Look at the *context* of the word, the words which come before and after it. Is the word used as another way of *expressing* something that has already been said or described? In the last sentence 'express' has almost the same meaning as 'say'. Writers often repeat themselves in order to get their *point* across.
2. See whether the word *occurs* elsewhere in the text. Its meaning in another sentence may be easier to guess because you have more *clues*.
3. Look at the kind of word it is – *noun*, adjective, etc. How does it *relate to* the other words in the sentence?
4. *Split* the word *up* into parts that you know. Take, for example, the word 'unsatisfactory'. You may never have seen this word before, but if you break it down into the parts *'un-satisfact-ory'* you will quickly understand its meaning. The *prefix* *'un'* describes the absence of a quality; *'satisfact-'* reminds you of *'satisfaction'* or *'satisfy'*; *'-ory'* is the suffix of many adjectives. (You'll find a list of common prefixes and *suffixes* in Appendix C).
5. Once you have guessed the meaning of a word check if it *makes sense* in the sentence.

wahrscheinlich
eilen
erschließen
Bedeutung
Aufgabe; raten
Zusammenhang
ausdrücken
Standpunkt
vorkommen
Hinweis
Substantiv
Bezug haben
aufteilen
Vorsilbe
befriedigen
Nachsilbe
Sinn machen

BSE or the mad cow disease

OUR STORY: Nothing left to eat

THE ARTICLE: Our mad cow was a Swiss import, claim Germans

Whet your appetite

Let's face it: "You are what you eat." Well, in the case of the mad cows that is a pretty depressing statement. A lot of our food is somehow polluted or genetically manipulated. Where will it all lead to? Maybe you don't care, like George Burns who said: "I personally stay away from natural foods. At my age I need all the preservatives I can get."

Time for a smile

The difference between vitamin and hormone is that you cannot hear vitamins.
Do-Ping, coach of the Chinese female olympic team

Americans will eat garbage provided you sprinkle it liberally with ketchup.
Henry Miller

McDonald's in Tokyo is a terrible revenge for Pearl Harbour.
S.I. Hayakawa

(*) Nothing left to eat

Mick Disney (**M**) meets Amy Fernando (**A**), both trainers from Personal Executive Language Consultants in Heidelberg, for a meal.

A: Haven't seen you for a long time, Mick. There's a rumour around that you're trying to become a golf pro.

M: Me, no, no, no, not good enough for that yet. No, I've just been avoiding you really. Ha ha, only a joke really.

A: Hey, Mick, watch it, will you. So when are you leaving? We've all had our suspicions.

M: Leaving what?

A: Leaving Germany. Your girlfriend told me you want to go back and live with her.

M: Oh my god, no. I mean, of course, she's nice. Too young. Amazing how stories get around.

A: Don't deny it, Mick! You can't endure anything about Germany.

M: Well, the food's okay. I'm going to have a great big steak. What about you?

A: You know I'm a vegetarian. Breeding all those animals for greedy humans. Ughhh!

M: This is a German steak from a German cow – best in the world.

A: That's just boasting! They've got BSE, too. I've been reading an article about it.

M: But there's no mad cow disease here. I'm sure they've got a cow purity law like for the beer.

A: Oh no, Mick. There've been several cases circulating around. There was a case of BSE with a cow called Anita. They said it came from Switzerland. But then the Swiss scientist proved that it had no genetic connections to any Swiss cow. Enjoy your meal.

M: What sort of a world is it, cows with BSE, salmon with salmonella, pigs with swine fever? Thank god I've got my beer.

A: So you didn't read about the bacteria in the beer pipes? Perhaps we should ban that, too. Don't get worked up about it anyway.

M: No pleasure in life any more!

Word watch

Task 1: Scanning for keywords

Find the words in the dialogue that have almost the same meaning.

information, a mixture of truth and untruth	*r* . . . . .
say arrogant things about oneself	*b* . . . .
stand, suffer or tolerate	*e* . . . . .
a feeling of mistrust	*s* . . . .
stories circulate	*g* . . *a* . . . . .

Task 2: In other words

Do you remember the way it was said in the dialogue?

That's only *making yourself important*.	That's just ....
Don't *say it's not true*, Mick.	Don't ...., Mick.
Raising all those animals for greedy humans.	.... all those animals for greedy humans.
There've been several cases *getting* around.	There've been several cases .... around.
You can't *tolerate* anything about Germany.	You can't .... anything about Germany.

Task 3: Complete the business idioms: One verb – five idioms

---- {
- a message around
- worked up
- a message across
- down to business
- under control

Word power

Task 4: Wordfinder's corner

Read the article on page 95 first before you do these exercises.

Find a word that has the opposite meaning

experts *accepted* claims	experts .... claims
lose one's reputation	.... one's reputation
weaken suspicions	.... suspicions

Find a word that has a similar meaning

home-bred cattle	.... cattle
give full explanation	.... full explanation
keep one's reputation	.... one's reputation
a *controversial* BSE case	a .... BSE case
clearly under-reported	.... under-reported
efforts to *lift* a ban	.... to .... a ban

Task 5: A little newspaper grammar

Articles have to be to the point. That is why journalists use short cuts. Do you remember how these sentences are shortened in the article?

Long sentence	Shortened sentence
a beast that was called Anita	a beast ....
a cow that was infected with BSE	a cow .... with BSE
has been found in Bavaria	found in Bavaria
an animal which was imported from Switzerland	an animal .... from Switzerland

Time for a smile

Notice in an Egyptian hotel: "The water in this establishment is completely hygienic – it has all been passed by the manager."

Task 6: Guesswork

1. The Swiss say they found no *genetic match* with other members of Anita's family.
   A. genetische Übereinstimmung
   B. Erbmaterial
   C. genetischen Fingerabdruck

2. Germany will have to provide a full explanation of the cow's origins if it is to avoid *cover-up claims*.
   A. Deckungsansprüche
   B. Schadenersatzforderungen
   C. Behauptungen, es würde etwas vertuschen

3. We will have to *sort* all this *out* as the stories are beginning to get around.
   A. aussortieren **B.** aufklären **C.** beweisen

4. Germany has *led opposition* to all attempts to *ease* the 23-month-old worldwide ban on British beef exports.
   A. die Opposition anführen **A.** erleichtern
   B. ging in die Opposition **B.** aufheben
   C. Opposition zulassen **C.** lockern

5. Cases of BSE on the Continent have been *under-reported*.
   A. verschwiegen **B.** untertrieben
   C. von der Presse vernachlässigt

6. There seems to be freedom from BSE in *home-bred cattle.*
   A. inländische Rinderzucht
   B. importierte Rinder
   C. heimische Schlachtungen

Our mad cow was a Swiss import, claim Germans

Germany's claim to have had no cases of mad cow disease in domestically bred cattle is being questioned in Brussels following an argument with Switzerland over a beast called Anita, writes Toby Helm.

The European Commission has asked for full details of the case after Swiss experts denied German claims that a cow infected with BSE found in Bavaria was Anita, an animal imported from Switzerland in 1995.

After carrying out tests on the dead animal's brain, the Swiss say they found no genetic match with other members of Anita's family, including her father.

Senior officials in Brussels say Germany will have to provide a full explanation of the cow's origins if it is to retain its record as a nation with no native cases of BSE and avoid cover-up claims.

Suspicions grew as strong rumours circulated in the Commission's agriculture directorate of another disputed BSE case in Germany. One senior EU official said: "We will have to sort all this out as the stories are beginning to get around."

The Anita case will be of great interest in Britain, which has had to endure German boasts about its freedom from BSE in home-bred cattle since the mad cow crisis broke. Germany has led opposition to all attempts to ease the 23-month-old worldwide ban on British beef exports.

Only six cases of BSE have been found in Germany and the authorities insist that all were in imported cattle. Five were in cows imported from Britain and the sixth, the Germans claimed, was Anita, the Swiss cow.

But the Swiss veterinary authorities said that the German information had been incorrect.

The dispute will strengthen suspicions among veterinary experts that cases of BSE on the Continent have been grossly under-reported.

Weekly Telegraph, 11–17 March, 1998

Time for a smile

I'm not a vegetarian because I love animals; I'm a vegetarian because I hate plants. *A.W. Brown*

Digesting the article

Task 7: Did you get the meaning?

Are these statements facts (F) or claims (C)?

	F	C
1. Six BSE cows have been found in Germany.		
2. No link between Anita and any Swiss cow has been found.		
3. BSE cows have been under-reported in Europe.		
4. Anita was an import from Switzerland.		
5. There are no home-bred BSE cows in Germany.		

Word aid

amazing	erstaunlich, verblüffend
attempt	Versuch, Anstrengung
authorities	Behörden
avoid	aus dem Weg gehen, (ver-)meiden
ban on exports	Exportverbote
beast	Tier
beef	Rindfleisch
beer pipes	Bier-, Zapfleitungen
boast	prahlen, angeben
boasts	prahlerische Behauptungen
brain	Gehirn
break, broke, broken	ausbrechen, brechen
breed, bred, bred	züchten
cattle	Rinder
claim (n)	Anspruch, Behauptung
claim (v)	behaupten, beanspruchen
cover-up	Vertuschung
crisis broke	die Krise brach aus
deny	leugnen, abstreiten
disease	Krankheit, Seuche
dispute	Streit, Zwist
disputed case	strittiger, umstrittener Fall
domestically bred	aus heimischer Zucht
ease ban on exports	Exportverbote lockern

endure	ertragen, aushalten
EU (European Union)	Europäische Union
find, found, found	finden
garbage	Abfall
get around	sich verbreiten
greedy	gierig
grossly	stark, grob, gröblich
grow, grew, grown	wachsen
humans	Menschen
in home-bred cattle	im Inland gezüchtete Rinder
infect	infizieren
insist (on)	bestehen, beharren (auf)
lead opposition	Opposition, Widerstand anführen
liberally	großzügig
mad cow disease	BSE
match, genetic ~	genetische Gemeinsamkeiten
meal	Mahlzeit
origins	Herkunft
pass water	Wasser lassen, freigeben, prüfen
preservatives	Konservierungsmittel
pro	Profi
provide	liefern
provided	vorausgesetzt
purity law	Reinheitsgesetz
question	in Frage stellen
retain one's record	seinen Ruf behalten
revenge	Rache
rumour	Gerücht
salmon	Lachs
scientist	Wissenschaftler
senior official	höhere(r) Beamter(r)
short cut	Abkürzung
sort out	aufklären
suspicion	Verdacht
swine fever	Schweinepest
under-reported	in der Presse wenig beachtet
veterinary authorities	Veterinärämter

Buba and the Euro

OUR STORY: Looking on the black side
THE ARTICLE: Welcome to Euroland

Whet your appetite

Well, money isn't everything in life, but it does keep you in touch with your children. "The softer the currency in a foreign country is, the harder the toilet paper," said a travelling economist who spent his holiday in Paris. European currencies will disappear, but whether the Euro will be as hard as French toilet paper remains to be seen. Practically everything about it is vague. We don't know what will happen to our savings, our insurance and the exchange rate of the Euro. Actually we don't even know which countries will meet the criteria. Our governments are pulling wool over our eyes.

Time for a smile

All the great economic ills the world has known this century can be directly traced back to the London School of Economics.
N.M. Perrera

Economy is cutting down other people's wages.
J.B. Morton

(*) Looking on the black side

Haron (**H**) from Pakistan and Nocktavia (**N**) from Germany, a married couple who run an Indian restaurant in Heidelberg, are discussing the question of the Euro.

N: I know it's bad in our business at the moment, but it'll be better when we have monetary union.

H: Monetary union? It's a complete flop. Do you think that's the remedy for everything, for all our problems?

N: It's no good gnashing your teeth about the Euro. At least it might solve some of our troubles.

H: I'm afraid not. It'll be a burden for all of us. We're all going to lose. There'll be more taxes everywhere. Germany's full of disquiet already.

N: Well, all relationships call for an element of give and take. And so will monetary union. Things would only get worse if we let too many weak countries in. In that case we'd have to pay for Greece and Turkey.

H: What on earth are you talking about? If a country wants to have the Euro it must qualify. It has to pass tests. And Germany doesn't pass them, either. The Bundesbank has checked all the countries. The implications are that only four or five countries qualify.

N: Which are they? Holland, France, Belgium, and Sweden?

H: Not at all. It's France, Luxembourg, Britain and maybe Denmark, Finland and Ireland. Germany doesn't. Moreover it has persistent problems with its unemployment.

N: So if this convergence doesn't work properly we should keep our strong, hard currency. Why give it up then?

H: Which strong, hard currency? The Deutschmark? Due to the rigid system here the Deutschmark has become soft. It's lost about thirty per cent against the British pound in two years.

N: Listen, Haron, if you don't like Germany, why do you stay here?

H: Good question.

Word watch

Task 1: Scanning for keywords

Find the words in the dialogue that have almost the same meaning.

money of a country	c . . . .
a coming together of things	c . . . .
something hard and inflexible	r . . . .
an idea or action which totally fails	f . . .
group of countries with a central government	u . . . .

Task 2: In other words

Do you remember the way it was said in the dialogue?

It'll be better when we have the *single currency*.	It'll be better when we have ....
The *signs are* that only four or five countries qualify.	The .... are that only four or five countries qualify.
Germany has *continual* problems with its unemployment.	Germany has .... problems with its unemployment.

Task 3: Complete the business idioms: One verb – five idioms

---- {
- up one's currency
- careful consideration (to)
- someone the sack
- and take
- out false information

Time for a smile

A German businessman entered a Swiss bank. He looked carefully around, went to the reception desk and whispered: "I want to invest 300,000 marks." – "You needn't whisper," said the bank clerk, "poverty is nothing to be ashamed of."

(P) Word power

Task 4: Wordfinder's corner

Read the article on page 102 first before you do these exercises.

Find a word that has the opposite meaning.

overstatement ....
quiet ....
temporary ....
flexibility ....
success ....

Find a word that has a similar meaning.

important ....
single currency ....
deliver a *judgement* ....
adequate warnings ....
finally ....
have *consequences* ....

Task 5: Guided translation

Some of the solutions to **task 4** will help you in this task.

1. [*Beitritt*] into monetary union will have [*bedeutende wirtschaftliche Auswirkungen/Folgen*].
2. The Buba [*sprach ihr Urteil*] on the birth of the Euro.
3. The document is a [*Meisterwerk der Untertreibung*].
4. If the Euro is a [*furchtbare Pleite*] then the Buba can [*hervorholen*] its document and say: "We told you so."
5. Measures with a [*vorübergehenden Effekt*] have been used by Italy and France to enable them to meet Maastricht reference values.
6. [*Anhaltende]* unemployment reflects rigidities which are a [*Dauerbelastung*] for the future [*Stabilitätspolitik*].

Buba's welcome to verdict on Euroland

And the Bundesbank looked at economic and monetary union and it saw that it was not so good. And the Bundesbank spoke: "Entry into monetary union will have significant economic implications which must be given careful consideration when the decision is taken. The selection of the participants ultimately remains a political decision."

With these words, the Bundesbank (Buba) delivered its verdict on the birth of the Euro. The document is a masterpiece of understatement that protects the Buba's reputation whatever happens. If the Euro is a terrible flop then the Buba can pull out its document and say: "We told you so." On the other hand, if the Euro is a success, the bank can claim the credit. It has signalled the appropriate warnings and puts the pressure on governments to take remedial action.

Much gnashing of teeth will have gone into the drafting of the Bundesbank's opus. But readers did not have to delve deeply between the lines to recognise the Bundesbank's extreme disquiet. It provided its own chart of how far countries are from the convergence criteria – and more ammunition besides:

- Page 13: very high and persistent unemployment throughout the Union (except Britain) reflects rigidities which are a long-term burden for the future stability policy.
- Page 15: government financial positions present a very divided picture. Measures with a temporary effect have been used by Italy and France to enable them to meet Maastricht reference values.
- Page 16: only four member states meet the Maastricht debt ratio (Finland, France, Luxembourg and Britain).
- Page 19: Denmark, Finland, Ireland, Luxembourg and the UK have achieved a sustainable fiscal position.

The European, 30 March–5 April 1998, Marc Champion and Eric Culp, Brussels & Frankfurt; abridged

Digesting the article

Task 6: Scanning for hard words

Which word in the article shows that ...

A. unemployment *goes on and on*? *p.........*
B. a country's position *can be kept at the same level*? *s..........*
C. choosing participants is *finally* a political decision? *u.........*
D. it is the Buba's *life work?* *o...*

Task 7: Did you get the meaning?

Are these statements true (T) or false (F)?

1. The Buba made a clear decision about the Euro. ☐ ☐
2. The Buba took some risks with its verdict. ☐ ☐
3. The Buba had some problems arriving at its comment. ☐ ☐
4. Britain has low unemployment because it is flexible. ☐ ☐

Task 8: Sensing style

Some phrases in the article are allusions (Anspielungen) to the Bible.

Are they allusions to the Bible?	**Yes**	**No**
1. There was much gnashing of teeth.	☐	☐
2. The bank can claim credit ...	☐	☐
3. And the Buba spoke ...	☐	☐
4. And the Buba looked, and saw it was no good.	☐	☐

Ⓥ Word aid

account	Konto
achieve	erreichen
ammunition	Munition
appropriate warnings	angemessene Warnungen
ashamed, be ~ about	sich schämen für
bank statement	Bankauszug
bank with	Bankgeschäfte machen mit
birth	Geburt
burden	Last, Belastung
chart	Diagramm
claim the credit	das Verdienst für sich beanspruchen
convergence	Annäherung, Konvergenz
credit something to an account	einem Konto etwas gutschreiben
debt ratio	Verschuldungsrate
decision, take a ~	eine Entscheidung fällen
deliver a verdict	ein Urteil verkünden
delve between the lines	zwischen den Zeilen herauslesen
disquiet	Unruhe, Besorgnis
draft an opus	ein Opus, Werk entwerfen
enable	in die Lage versetzen
exchange rate	Wechselkurs
fiscal position	steuerliche Situation, Lage
flop	Reinfall, Pleite
give careful consideration (to)	etwas sorgfältig überlegen
give someone the sack	jemanden entlassen
give up one's currency	seine Währung aufgeben
gnash one's teeth	mit den Zähnen knirschen
implications	Folgen, Auswirkungen
monetary union	Währungsunion
overdraw one's account	sein Konto überziehen
participant	Teilnehmer
pass a test	einen Test bestehen
pepper	pfeffern, hier: würzen
persistent	anhaltend, hartnäckig
poverty	Armut

pull the wool over someone's eyes	jemandem Sand in die Augen streuen
put pressure on	Druck ausüben auf
qualify	sich qualifizieren
reference values	Vergleichswerte
remain	bleiben
remedial action	Abhilfemaßnahmen
remedy	Heilmittel, Lösung
reputation	Ruf, Ansehen
rigid	starr, inflexibel
run a restaurant	ein Restaurant führen
selection	Auswahl
significant	bedeutsam, wichtig
sustainable	aufrechterhaltbar, durchhaltbar
trace back to	zurückverfolgen bis
ultimately	letztlich
understatement	Untertreibung

Time for a smile

Groucho Marx hated the meaningless phrases that pepper business letters. Once, having received a letter from his bank manager with the standard, "If I can be of any service to you, please do not hesitate to call on me", ending, he wrote back:

Dear Sir,

The best thing you can do to be of service to me is to steal some money from the account of one of your richer clients and credit it to mine.

My bank sent me a bank statement last week saying that I was seven hundred pounds overdrawn. I reacted promptly. I immediately wrote them a cheque for the money.

Nike versus Adidas

OUR STORY: The power of advertising

THE ARTICLE: World Cup's battle of the boots

Whet your appetite

Why advertising? Well, business without advertising is like throwing kisses to a girl in the dark. You know what you're doing, but nobody else does. Industry produces more variety than we really need. Not necessarily more things, but more variety. That's where advertising comes in. Do you really need two different pairs of jogging shoes? Yes, if you believe the TV spot, then you must wear one pair in cold weather and another pair in warm weather. That's what our article is all about.

Time for a smile

In writing a patent medicine advertisement, first convince the reader that he has the disease he is reading about; second, that it is curable. *R. F. Fenno, 1908*

Any small thing can be made large by the right kind of advertising.

Sign in a shop window: Our clothes not only make girls slim, they also make men look round.

(*) The power of advertising

Tony (T) and Mick Disney (M) are discussing their health problems at the new Irish pub in the old city of Heidelberg:

T: So if you really want to get fit you have to jog and swim and walk a lot. You have to step up all your body-movement.

M: Oh, I'm not into this power walking thing. I know there's a boom in it, but I find it stupid.

T: I've been listening to a series of broadcasts on the radio which said that basically you have to square up to your own real needs. Set your calory level, fix your periods of swimming and jogging, and you'll be the beneficiary of your own self-discipline.

M: Wow, that was some speech. Just for an audience of one person, namely myself. Okay, I'm going out to buy some Adidas jogging kit immediately.

T: Hey, slowly now. Why Adidas?

M: Well, it's a well-known make. You know all the best people are wearing it.

T: And what about Nike?

M: Well, Nike is good, too, but Adidas is on every TV programme. Every viewer knows the name.

T: You've been ambushed by advertising. It's the science of arresting your intelligence long enough to get money from it. It's nothing to do with quality. More to do with distribution.

M: Well, they seem to be a sponsor for the World Cup. The world's best teams will be playing in it.

T: And Nike has sponsored Brazil and some others.

M: In that case I'd better get no-name equipment.

Word watch

Task 1: Scanning for keywords

Find the words in the dialogue that have almost the same meaning.

listeners	*a . . . .*
equipment	*k . .*
programme on the air	*b . . . .*
someone who watches TV	*v . . . . .*
support a product with money	*s . . . . . .*
someone who profits by an action	*b . . . . y*

Task 2: In other words

Do you remember the way it was said in the dialogue?

You have to *look after* your own real needs.	You have to .... to your own real needs.
You've been *tricked* by advertising.	You've been .... by advertising.
I know there's a *lot of demand* in this market.	I know there's a .... in this market.

Task 3: Complete the business idioms: *sign* and *step*

Choose the verb and a preposition that fits the idiom.

away, down, over, in, up, into

1. The old chairman stepped .... because of the company's losses.
2. The bank stepped .... to save the company from bankruptcy.
3. John, one of the directors, stepped ...... the old chairman's shoes.
4. He managed to step .... production again.
5. John signed .... three new production managers.
6. He signed .... some of the buildings for use as offices.
7. He had to sign .... his right to the money.

Ⓟ Word power

Read the article on page 111. Then come back and try these exercises without looking at the wordlist.

Task 4: Wordfinder's corner

the *competition* is bitter	.... is bitter
supporter of a club	.... of a club
set up a football village	.... a football village
six international *teams*	six international ....
get ready to fight	.... to fight
react by doing something	.... by doing something

Task 5: Words in context

If you have solved our tasks you will have no problems to fill the gaps.

1. They are .... to fight for the largest .... on the planet.
2. It has also sponsored the .... of nine teams.
3. Adidas will .... a football village under the Eiffel Tower.
4. Nike has .... six international ....
5. Adidas has .... Paul Gascoigne, Paul Ince and David Beckham.
6. Nike has .... by planning a site outside the city.

Time for a smile

Noticing that just before the football game started, the teams gathered together and prayed briefly, a fan, seated next to a minister, asked what he thought would happen if both teams prayed with equal faith and fervour. "In that event," replied the minister, "I imagine the Lord would simply sit back and enjoy one fine game of football."

My son has the making of a football hooligan. He threw a bottle at the referee yesterday. I wouldn't mind, but he broke the screen.

Task 6: Guesswork

Guess what the words in *italics* mean.

1. Nike is *determined* to *muscle in* among the official sponsors.
   A. unschlüssig B. entschlossen C. zuversichtlich
   A. get in by force B. offer training C. give money

2. If those viewers go out and buy football boots that *constitutes* a boom.
   A. consume B. convince C. result in

3. Nike managed *virtually* to ruin the Olympics for the official sponsors by *ruthless* advertising.
   A. fast B. scheinbar C. eigentlich
   A. irresponsible B. uncaring C. clever

4. The Olympic Committee ordered that all poster sites in the city be bought up and fairly *distributed*.
   A. spread B. shared C. spared

5. We are going to *ambush* their ambush by having our own stunts and tricks.
   A. beat B. deceive C. lie in wait for

6. Nike has *responded* by planning a site on the *outskirts* of the city.
   A. reagieren B. nachgeben C. sich zurückziehen
   A. neighbourhood B. center C. suburb

7. Nike will try to steal its glory by *planning a series of 'counter-stunts*
   A. react by spectacular publicity campaigns
   B. plan spectacular demonstration with stuntmen
   C. react by changing its marketing strategy

World Cup's battle of the boots

Adidas and Nike are squaring up for their big match in France. Alison Boshoff reports.

The prize, as ever, is colossal. The rivalry is bitter. Adidas and Nike are squaring up to fight for the hearts and minds of possibly the largest audience on the planet during the World Cup Finals.

FIFA says the 1998 World Cup will be broadcast to 195 countries, with each game being seen by 500 million people worldwide.

If a fraction of those viewers go out and buy football boots after the tournament, that constitutes a boom. And both Adidas and Nike are determined that they should be the beneficiaries of any increased competition for the game.

Adidas is among 12 official sponsors of the tournament, but it is feared that it could suffer as a result of a determined campaign by Nike, which is determined to muscle in.

In Atlanta last year, Nike managed virtually to ruin the Olympics for the official sponsors by ruthless advertising and by exploiting its star names.

The strategy was so effective that the International Olympic Committee has had to step in to try to protect official sponsors in Athens in 2004 from Nike by ordering that all poster sites in the city be bought up and fairly distributed.

Adidas is so sure that Nike will try to steal its glory that it is planning a series of "counter-stunts" in addition to traditional advertising and marketing.

"We have bought all our advertising and posters but there are other tricks that can be played," a spokesman said.

"We are going to ambush their ambush by having our own stunts and tricks."

Each company has made all of the obvious moves. Adidas will erect a football village under the Eiffel Tower. Nike has responded by planning a site on the outskirts of the city.

Adidas has signed up Paul Gascoigne, Paul Ince and David Beckham. It has also sponsored the kit of nine teams, including Germany, France and Spain.

Nike has sponsored six international squads, including the favourites, Brazil. The battle has been joined because of the success of the 1994 event.

Daily Telegraph, 4 December 97

Digesting the article

Task 7: Scanning for figures

To how many countries will the 1998 World Cup be broadcast? ....

How many million viewers will watch each game worldwide? ....

How many official sponsors will be admitted to the 1998 World Cup? ....

How many international teams has Nike sponsored? ....

How many international teams has Adidas sponsored? ....

Task 8: Did you get the meaning?

Are these statements true (T) or false (F)?

1. Nike and Adidas target their campaigns at the spectators who come to the World Cup finals. ☐☐
2. Nike and Adidas are among the twelve official sponsors of the World Cup. ☐☐
3. The Olympic Committee will prevent Nike from buying up all poster sites in Paris. ☐☐
4. Nike is going to erect a football village in Paris. ☐☐

Word aid

addition, in ~ to	zusätzlich
ambush	Hinterhalt, auflauern
audience	Zuhörerschaft, Publikum
beneficiary	Nutznießer
broadcast	Radiosendung
constitute	hier: herbeiführen, bedeuten
convince	überzeugen
counter-stunt	spektakuläre Gegenaktion
curable	heilbar
determined	entschlossen
distribute	verteilen

equipment	Ausrüstung
event	Ereignis, Veranstaltung
exploit	ausbeuten, ausnutzen
faith	Glaube, Vertrauen
fervour	Inbrunst
fraction	Bruchteil
glory	Ruhm
join the battle	den Kampf aufnehmen
kit	Ausrüstung
level	Niveau, Leistungsstand
loss	Verlust
move	Schritt, Maßnahme
muscle in	rücksichtslos eindringen
obvious	offensichtlich
outskirts	Außenbezirk, Vorort
poster site	hier: Werbeflächen
pray briefly	kurz beten
protect	(be-)schützen
referee	Schiedsrichter
respond	reagieren, antworten
rivalry	Rivalität, Konkurrenzkampf
ruthless	mitleidlos, unbarmherzig
screen	Fernsehschirm
sign away	mit einem Federstrich verzichten
sign over	vertraglich übertragen
sign up someone	jemanden unter Vertrag nehmen
site	Gelände
squad	Truppe
square up to	anpacken, in Angriff nehmen
step down	zurücktreten
step in	einschreiten, einspringen
step into someone's shoes	in jemandes Fußstapfen treten
step up production	die Produktion ankurbeln
stupid	dumm
suburb	Vorort
tournament	Turnier
TV spot	Werbung im Fernsehen
viewer	Zuschauer, Betrachter
virtually	praktisch, fast

✔ Boost your reading skills 6: Facts about speed reading

A person reading a 90,000 word book at 900 words per minute finishes in an hour and forty minutes. The *average* reader, who manages about 250 words per minute, takes six hours. Let us first be clear about what speed reading is. It is completely different from the technique you learnt at school.

1. It is not just skimming and scanning a text or a book.
2. Speeds of above 500 words per minute are possible.
3. Speed reading is not unnatural.
4. The fast reader does not *comprehend*, understand or *appreciate* less.
5. Higher speeds don't produce lower concentration.
6. *Reading with your finger* does not slow you down.
7. You *needn't* always read page 4 before you read page 5.
8. Speed reading should not *accompanied* by a 'hidden voice', a tendency to *pronounce* the printed words *silently.*
9. Each word should be read as a *whole unit.*
10. The reading is not *executed* from left to right line by line, until the page is finished.
11. Don't look up any words you do not understand.
12. Problems or difficult areas in a book needn't be *dealt with* before moving on.
13. Notes needn't be *neat* and written in sentence form.
14. You needn't *remember* 100% of what you read.

We'll show you step by step how to speed reading.

durchschnittlich
erfassen, verstehen
hier: genießen
mit dem Finger 'lesen'; nicht brauchen
begleiten
aussprechen
still
ganze Einheit
ausführen
behandeln
ordentlich, sauber
erinnern

Transparent man

(*) OUR STORY: Big brother is watching you

(!) THE ARTICLE: Handprint passports

Whet your appetite

What about our privacy? The computer is creeping into every part of our lives. It seems we are becoming nothing more than a series of numbers on magnetic strips or in some software somewhere. What about our personal data protection? This chapter is concerned with another example of putting us all "on file".

Time for a smile

Bridget O'Leary was trying to cash a cheque in a Dublin bank. "Can you identify yourself, madam?" asked the clerk. "Certainly," said Bridget, reached into her handbag, took out a little mirror, looked in it and declared confidently, "Yes, it's me all right. I'd recognise me anywhere."

(*) Big brother is watching you

Dave Makeit (**D**) and James Kelly[1] (**J**), both working for SASL (Sports Aids for the Slow Learner), discuss travel and new technology.

J: Oh dear me, I can't be doing with all this new technology. I don't carry credit cards and bank cards.

D: Hey man, cards make your life easier. They aim at cutting the need to waste time running to the bank.

J: My goodness, no. I couldn't trust all that. You never know what they're doing. They don't reveal what really happens to your money. When you give them permission to work with electronic cards, they gain access to every part of your life. Think of your civil liberties.

D: Mister, you're really unique. All this electronics is state of the art.

J: As long as I've got the choice not to use this stuff I'll be happy.

D: Well, I've got some bad news for you, man. You don't have a choice. They're thinking of introducing electronic palm prints for people travelling to your native land. And if the system doesn't recognise your palm print, you don't get in. It's as simple as that.

J: You're not trying to tell me that they're going to do away with passports, are you?

D: You've got it. You swipe your card through and if it doesn't match your palm print, you're out, or should I say 'not in'.

J: I don't have to accept all this. It's all 'Big brother is watching you'.

D: Don't worry. Nobody could forge your palm print. It's too small.

J: Ha ha. Very funny. But in any case there are a lot of groups who are going to oppose this. If you ask me it's just another way of bringing in national identity cards.

D: Hey, dude, you Texans are hopelessly old-fashioned. Every other civilised country has had ID cards for years.

---

[1] Both characters are heroes in *Let's Go International. Business English rund um die Welt*, rororo 60267. A humorous story about cross-cultural differences.

Word watch

Task 1: Scanning for keywords

Find the words that have almost the same meaning.

be against something ....
illegally copy passports ....
most modern technology ....
make known secret plans ....

Task 2: In other words

Do you remember how they said it in the dialogue?

You Texans are *living in the past.*	You Texans are ...-.......... .
The system doesn't *accept* your palm print.	The system doesn't .... your palm print.
There's nobody quite like you.	You're ....

Task 3: Our business idioms: cut, do, carry

Can you match idiom with meaning?

1 cut the need to do it	**A** Pässe abschaffen
2 cut queues by a half	**B** Warteschlangen halbieren
3 do away with passports	**C** Kreditkarten besitzen
4 carry credit cards	**D** Löhne senken
5 cut wages	**E** etwas überflüssig machen
6 do business with	**F** Geschäfte machen mit

And now put the right idiom in the right context.

1. They are thinking of .... to be more competitive.
2. You've failed to .... your agreement to repay the bank loan.
3. The government can't .... with civil liberties.
4. He is not a frank and open character. If I were you I wouldn't .... him.

(P) Word power

Read the article on page 120. Then do these exercises.

Task 4: Wordfinder's corner

Find a word that has almost the same meaning as the words in *italics*.

pay with *plastic money*	pay by ....
recognise a handprint	.... a handprint
do away with civil liberties	.... civil liberties
get access to an establishment	.... access to an establishment
put one's hand against a screen	.... one's hand against a screen
shorten queues	.... queues

Find the opposite of the words in *italics*

do away with civil liberties	.... civil liberties
shorten queues	.... queues
keep plans *secret*	.... plans
be in favour of the system	.... the system
numbers will *fall* by 6 %	numbers will .... by 6 %

Task 5: Business words in context

Put some of the solutions into the dialogue below.

At the car showroom: Bob (**B**), salesman (**S**)

B: I saw your new Rolls Royce .... for the first time. I was very impressed with it. Your company has .... in my estimation. There are, however, a few things I'm not clear about.

S: Well, thank you for your support. I hope we can .... any doubt you still have about the Rolls.

B: There's one thing. Could you .... the price a bit?

S: Everything is possible, but it'll have to be a cash payment, no ....

B: And what about the maintenance? Will I be able to afford a Rolls?

S: Well, I'm afraid anybody who asks a question like that can't.

Task 6: Guesswork

Read the following article without looking at the wordlist.
Then come back and guess what the words in *italics* mean.

1. Based on palm-print recognition, it is *aimed at* doing away with traditional passports.
   A. designed to **B.** expected to **C.** used to

2. The system allows passengers through when they *swipe* a card containing matching details.
   A. strike **B.** show **C.** pass through

3. The new system *converts* the print into computerised code.
   A. creates **B.** rewrites **C.** translates

4. If the card has been stolen, the print will not *match* and alarms will *sound.*
   A. recognise **B.** fit **C.** identify
   A. ring **B.** cling **C.** sting

5. Civil liberties groups *are likely to* oppose the system.
   A. will probably **B.** will like to **C.** will certainly

Time for a smile: Found in newspapers

Prince Philip flew into London airport last night.
It is hoped to have it rebuilt by the end of the week.

Twenty-five-year friendship ends at altar

Father of 10 shot – Mistaken for rabbit

Man found dead in cemetery

Advert:
Shop assistant required – No objection to sex.
Situation vacant advertisement. *Looe, Cornwall. 1983*

Handprint passports

An identification system straight out of the pages of a spy thriller is to be tested at a British airport.

Based on palm-print recognition, it is aimed at doing away with traditional passports.

Passengers will place their hands against monitor screens, which will recognise their unique prints and allow them through when they swipe a card containing matching details.

Airport officials hope the new system will cut ever-lengthening queues at immigration control points. With the number of air passengers expected to rise by six per cent each year, they say the situation is becoming critical. Instead of a passport, passengers will carry a credit card-style swipe pass which identifies their handprint and carries other information about them.

The state-of-the-art method – already used to gain access to top-secret establishments – should allow passengers through immigration in 15 seconds.

Tim Flesher, the deputy head of the UK immigration service, revealed plans to test the system, probably at Heathrow Airport, this autumn.

He told the International Policy Review: 'We have to go in this direction. In 50 years time, a paper-based system will be hopelessly old-fashioned.'

IBM has developed the system which converts a traveller's print into a computerised code which is then placed on the magnetic strip of a piece of plastic. If the card has been stolen, or forged, the print will not match and alarms will sound.

Civil liberties groups are likely to oppose the system, which could be seen as a way of introducing national identity cards by the back door.

Martin Slade, general secretary of the Immigration Service Union, said it removed the vital element of human intuition.

David Norris, Daily Mail, 4 May 1998

❗ Digesting the article

Task 7: Scanning for figures

Expected rise in passenger numbers per year: ..... per cent
How long will it take to get through immigration using handprint passports? ..... seconds
In how many years will a paper-based system be out of date? in ..... years

Task 8: Guided note-taking practice

1. The new system is based on ....
2. The handprint is converted ....
3. The information is placed ....
4. A card contains ....

Task 9: Scanning for attitudes

1. Which words show the author's attitude towards the new system?
   A .... B ....
2. Which word shows the opinion of the airport officials to the increasing number of passengers?
3. What does Tim Flesher, deputy head of the UK Immigration service, think of paper-based systems?
4. Which phrase expresses the fear of civil liberties groups?

Time for a smile

My uncle, who had overdrawn his account by too much, received a sarcastic letter from his bank manager:
Dear Mr Kleinschroth,
I have noticed that your account is now overdrawn well over the limit and has been for some time. Can we please return to the original arrangement where you bank with us and not we bank with you?

Ⓥ Word aid

aim at	abzielen auf
carry a credit card	eine Kreditkarte haben, besitzen
carry out a plan	einen Plan ausführen
civil liberties groups	Bürgerrechtsbewegungen
confidently	zuversichtlich
contain	enthalten
convert	umwandeln
cut queues by a half	Warteschlangen halbieren
cut the ground from under someone's feet	jemandem den Boden unter den Füßen wegziehen
cut the need to do it	es überflüssig machen
cut the wages	die Löhne senken
deputy head	Vizechef
develop a system	ein System entwickeln
do away with passports	Pässe abschaffen
do business with	Geschäfte machen mit
establishment	Einrichtung, Institution
ever-lengthening queues	immer länger werdende Schlangen
forge	fälschen
gain access	Einlaß erhalten
handprint	Handabdruck
identity card	Personalausweis
immigration	Einwanderung
immigration control points	Schalter der Einwanderungskontrolle
likely, be ~ to do	wahrscheinlich tun werden
loan	Kredit, Darlehen
magnetic strip	Magnetstreifen
maintenance	Wartung, Unterhalt
matching details	übereinstimmende Einzelheiten
mistake (v)	verwechseln
mirror	Spiegel
objection	Einwand, Hinderungsgrund
old-fashioned	altmodisch
oppose the system	gegen das System sein

palm	Handfläche
print	hier: Abdruck
rabbit	Kaninchen
recognise	(wieder-)erkennen
recognition	Erkennung
remove	entfernen, beseitigen
reveal plans	Pläne enthüllen
rise in someone's estimation	in jemandes Achtung steigen
screen	Bildschirm
sound	ertönen, klingen
spy thriller	Spionageroman
state-of-the-art	Stand der Technik
straight	direkt, gerade
swipe a card	eine Karte durchziehen
unique	einmalig, einzigartig
vital	wesentlich
woodpecker	Specht

Time for a smile

Experts at the Pentagon were scratching their heads about what to do next. Their most complicated code had been cracked by seven teenagers using ordinary computers.

If builders built buildings the way programmers wrote programs, then the first woodpecker that came along would destroy civilisation.

I can't understand the fuss over computer pornography. Surely everybody has seen a computer without clothes on by now.

✔ Boost your reading skills 7: Reading with your fingers

Ordinary *reading skills* won't do in today's world because there is too much information and too little time to read it. If you read at the *average* speed of 250 words per minute, you won't be able to *take in* the facts you need to do well on the job.

Lesefertigkeiten · *Durchschnitts-* · *aufnehmen*

The slow reader

His eyes do not move *smoothly* over the page, but move in small *jerks* from word to word, pausing momentarily to take in a word or two before moving on. These hundreds and thousands of pauses take up most of the time and are not necessary for good *comprehension.*

gleichmäßig · *Sprung, Ruck* · *Verständnis*

The slow reader also loses time because he often *re-reads* words. He returns to words that have just been read and to words which the reader feels he has *missed* or misunderstood.

noch mal lesen · *überlesen*

The fast reader

He doesn't take in a word or a little more at a time but is able to take in three or more words in a *continuous* and flowing movement of his eyes. You can *practise* this using your fingers.

stetig · *üben*

Place your right hand flat on the page. Move the *tips* of your fingers along the line you're reading. At the end of the line, lift your fingers and then bring your hand back down to the beginning of the next line and so on.

Spitzen

Like a scanner your eye follows the *steady* movement of your hand. Try to *increase* the speed a little with every line. The steady underlining *motion* helps keep your eyes from stopping on single words or *terms* in the text.

stetig · *erhöhen* · *Bewegung* · *Ausdruck*

Motorcar misery

* OUR STORY: Managing the motorcar
! THE ARTICLE: Trouble in the company fleet

Whet your appetite

Do you know the difference between a pedestrian and a motorist? Well, the pedestrian is the one who has found a place to park his car. I'm against cars, I'm a convinced cyclist. Why? By the time you've considered the price of a car, the petrol consumption, the cost of maintenance, cost of your parking lot, the damage to the environment, not to speak of parking fines, speeding fines and other fines, you'll probably buy the cheapest model, namely the bicycle.

Time for a smile

I once bought a car designed for five people: one had to drive while the other four pushed.

I've got a two tone car – black and rust.

My car is so old and dilapidated that someone scrawled on it:
Rust in peace.

⊛ Managing the motorcar

Andrew Goodman[1] (**A**) visits his oldest friend, Conchita Gonzales (**C**), in Portugal. They are on their way to a fine fish dinner. Suddenly there is a 'pop, pop, pop' and the car stops.

C: Jesus Christ! What's happened now? I've got no power. The engine's stopped.

A: Quick! Pull to the side. Let's get out of the traffic.

C: The car's broken down despite the fact that it was checked last week at the garage.

A: (*Trying to start it*) Well, it's not working. Probably the alternator. We'll have to call out the mechanic.

C: But the car's always been so reliable. I could always depend on it in every situation.

A: It's five years old. Perhaps you should think about getting a new one.

C: Well, if I do I'll probably get a VW again. They're quite good really.

A: Listen, I've just been reading a report on car breakdowns not including punctures, flat batteries etc. VW has been struck off the list of reliable cars. Their performance has really deteriorated.

C: What should I buy then? I need a small, cheap car.

A: Perhaps you could get a small Mitsubishi. They have the least breakdowns.

C: Someone recommended I should buy a Citroën or an Alpha.

A: Well, they might look nice but that would really be the booby prize. They're the worst for breakdowns. You'd be paying out all the time.

C: Well, what would be the best?

A: Well, looking at all these holes in the road I reckon you should go for a second-hand tank.

C: Ha, ha, ha!

[1] Have you met Andrew Goodman? He is our hero in *How to Phone Effectively. Business English am Telefon*, rororo 60139

Word watch

Task 1: Scanning for keywords

Find the words in the dialogue that have almost the same meaning.

get worse and worse	*d . . . . e*
failure of a system	*b . . . . n*
flat tyre of a car or bike	*p . . . . . . e*

Task 2: In other words

Do you remember how it was said in the dialogue?

The car's always been so *dependable.*	The car's always been so ....
The car won't move another inch.	The car's ....
That would really be a *prize for the losers.*	That would really be the ....
VW has been *eliminated from* the list of reliable cars.	VW has been .... the list of reliable cars.

Task 3: One verb – five business idioms

Build the idiom and put it in the right sentence.

Basic verb: strike + trouble, a balance, a good bargain, for, off

1. Most cars strike .... during the first year.
2. VW has been struck .... the list of the most reliable cars.
3. Automobile workers are striking .... higher wages.
4. I struck .... I bought a second-hand Mitsubishi for $200.
5. Let's strike .... and come to a fair decision.

Ⓟ Word power

Read the article on page 130 first. Then come back and do these exercises.

Task 4: Wordfinder's corner

Find a word that has the same meaning as the words in *italics*.

have a breakdown	.... a breakdown
quality has *deteriorated*	quality has ....
make cars more *reliable*	make cars more ....
get into trouble	.... trouble
put a model *on the market*	.... a model
the most improved *brand*	the most improved ....

Find the opposite of the words in *italics*.

increase in performance	.... in performance
cars are becoming *reliable*	cars are becoming ....
a *worsening* compared with last year	an .... compared with last year
double (v) the breakdowns per year	.... the breakdowns per year

Task 5: Words in context

Use your solutions from **task 4** and fill in the gaps in the following sentences. Be careful to fit them grammatically.

1. Company cars are becoming more troublesome, with one in four models .... a breakdown.
2. The .... in performance comes despite claims from producers.
3. Saab almost .... its breakdown count.
4. The best company car on the road is now a Jaguar, with just seven breakdowns per 100 vehicles – an .... from 9.2 last year.
5. Second-place BMW .... from 7.1 last year to 8.2 in 1997.
6. Mercedes .... noticeably to 13.4 – which makes it less dependable than Fiat, Nissan and Honda.

Task 6: Car parts that may cause a breakdown

Can you match these parts of the car with the German translation?

1	accelerator	A	Vergaser
2	brake	B	Kupplung
3	clutch	C	Bremse
4	alternator	D	Lüfter
5	fan	E	Kühler
6	carburettor	F	Kolben
7	piston	G	Reifen
8	gear box	H	Gaspedal
9	tyre	I	Verteiler
10	radiator	J	Getriebe

Task 7: Guesswork

Read the following article without looking at the wordlist.
Then come back and guess what the words in *italics* mean.

1. This decline in performance comes *despite* repeated claims from manufacturers that modern technology is making models more reliable.
   A. trotz B. wegen C. veranlaßt durch

2. Lex did not include *call-outs* due to accidents, punctures or flat batteries that were the driver's fault.
   A. Rückrufe B. Notrufe C. Hilferufe

3. The most-improved *make* is Saab.
   A. category B. class C. brand

4. Alfa Romeo will be *disappointed* with its second-worst showing.
   A. unzufrieden B. enttäuscht C. überrascht

5. Examining the *records* of the 88,000 in its leasing fleet, Lex found that almost 22,000 had struck trouble during the 12-month period.
   A. Leistung B. Rekord C. Unterlagen

Trouble in the company fleet

Company cars are becoming more troublesome with one in four models in Lex's 1997 Reliability Survey suffering a breakdown – compared with one in five in the 1996 report. This decline in performance comes despite repeated claims from manufacturers that modern technology is making models more reliable.

Examining the records of the 88,000 L to R registration cars on its leasing fleet, Lex found that almost 22,000 had struck trouble during the 12-month period. Alternators, clutches and engine problems were the top causes of the breakdowns: Lex did not include call-outs due to accidents, punctures or flat batteries that were the driver's fault.

The most reliable overall is still a Mitsubishi, with only five breakdowns per 100, while the best company car on the road is now a Jaguar, with just seven breakdowns per 100 vehicles on the fleet – an improvement from 9.2 last year. Second-place BMW deteriorated from 7.1 last year to 8.2 in 1997, and Mercedes worsened noticeably to 13.4 – which makes it less dependable than Fiat, Nissan and Honda.

The most improved make is Saab, almost halving its breakdown count from 24.8 to 13.7, while the booby prize still goes to Citroën, nearly half of whose cars broke down during the survey period.

Not far behind are Ford, Renault, Rover and Vauxhall, but new entrant Alfa Romeo will be disappointed with its second-worst showing, especially as it prepares to launch its 156 model against quality German rivals.

Sunday Business, 15 February 1998

Digesting the article

Task 8: Working with the graph

In the following graph we have replaced some car manufacturers with dotted lines (...). Can you put them back?

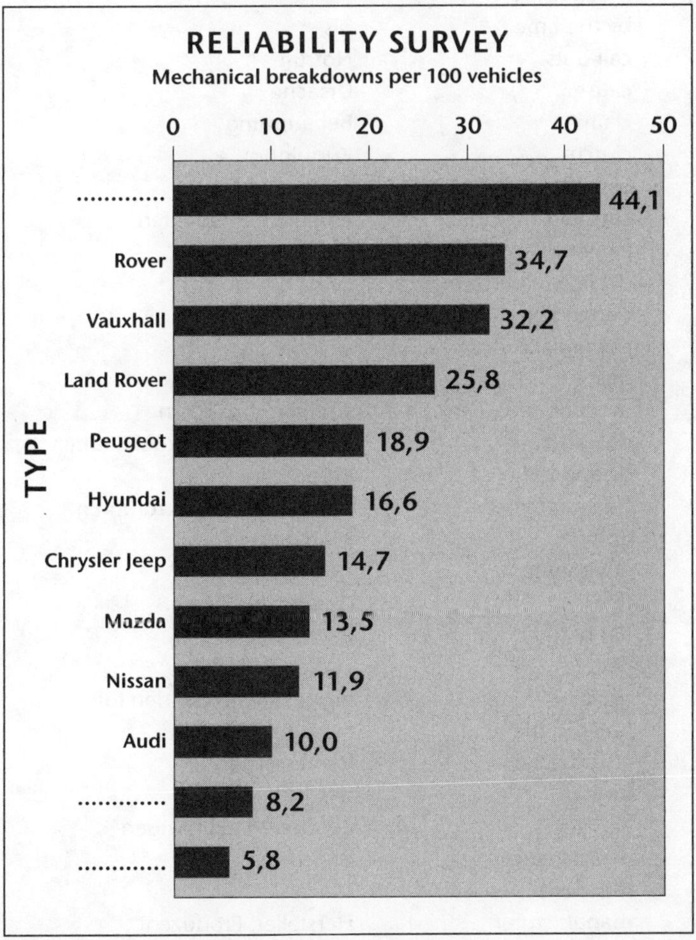

Ⓥ Word aid

alternator	Verteiler (im Auto)
become troublesome	zur Plage werden
bend	Kurve
booby prize	Trostpreis
breakdown	Panne
by the time	bis
call-outs	Notrufe
cause	Ursache
claim	Behauptung
clutch	Kupplung
company car	Firmenwagen
consider	erwägen, betrachten
convince	überzeugen
decline in performance	Leistungsrückgang
depend on	sich verlassen auf
dependable	zuverlässig
despite	trotz
deteriorate	sich verschlechtern
dilapidated	klapprig, heruntergekommen
disappoint	enttäuschen
due to accidents	auf Unfälle zurückzuführen
engine	Maschine
environment	Umwelt
fine	Geldbuße
flat battery	leere Batterie
fleet	Flotte, Fuhrpark
go for	hier: sich entscheiden für
holes in the road	Schlaglöcher
improvement	Verbesserung
instead	anstatt
launch	auf den Markt bringen
maintenance	Wartung
make (n)	Marke
manufacturer	Hersteller, Produzent

misery	Elend
new entrant	neu auf der Liste
parking lot	Parkplatz
pedestrian	Fußgänger
performance	Leistung
petrol consumption	Benzinverbrauch
puncture	Reifenpanne, Plattfuß
push	schieben
reckon	meinen, glauben
record	Bericht, Leistungsbilanz
registration cars	Neuanmeldungen
reliable	zuverlässig
rust	Rost
showing	hier: Ergebnis
speeding	Geschwindigkeitsübertretung, Raserei
strike a balance	den Saldo, die Bilanz ziehen
strike a bargain	ein Geschäft, einen Handel abschließen
strike for / against	streiken für / gegen
strike oil	auf Öl stoßen
strike someone off a list	jemanden von einer Liste streichen
strike, struck, struck	schlagen
strike trouble	auf Probleme stoßen
strike up a conversation	eine Unterhaltung anknüpfen
survey period	Zeitraum der Marktübersicht
traffic	Verkehr
worsen noticeably	sich merklich verschlechtern

Time for a smile

Policeman: "When I saw you coming round that bend I thought: 'Forty-five at least.'"
Woman motorist: "Well, I always look older in this hat."

✔ Boost your reading skills 8: About hand and mouth

Your hand

You remember 'Reading with your fingers?' Don't skip from word to word. Find a *smooth* rhythm. You may find *difficulty* in speeding up the movement of your hand because you are *used to* your old reading habit. Don't give up – *practice* is everything.
Don't stop at *unknown* words. With English texts you can use a pencil or a marker instead of your hand. Mark the words and *look* them *up* when you have finished reading.

ruhig, stetig
Schwierigkeit
gewöhnt an
Übung
unbekannt
nachschlagen

Your mouth

A *major* reading problem is the tendency to form the words with your mouth, to say them with your 'inner *voice*'. Read with your eyes only.
However, you might try to say out loud the *key words* that you see. It doesn't really *matter* which words you choose. The point here is to keep your voice 'busy', to *remove* it from the reading process. But as you talk out loud, don't allow your eye movement to slow down.

wichtig, größer
Stimme
Schlüsselwörter
wichtig sein
ausschalten

Practice

Take a *stop watch* and a German newspaper. Read an article at your normal speed without using the speed reading technique. When you have finished *note the time.*
Then read the article using the hand-movement technique and note your time again.
Read it a third time *increasing* the speed of your hand. This time say out loud any words that you think are important. Keep practising.

Stoppuhr
die Zeit nehmen
erhöhen

Chapter 15

The best meals in the skies

OUR STORY: Swissair to hang up flying suits

THE ARTICLE: Swissair starts to sing for its supper

Whet your appetite

The famous old Swiss airline is moving into new fields to increase its turnover and profits. They have come to the conclusion that flying passengers is not necessarily good business, especially now with air fares going down to rock bottom. Read on to find out what the Swiss are good at.

Time for a smile

"Personally, I don't believe in supersonic oversea transport."
"Because you're conservative?"
"No. Because I lisp."

At the travel agency:
"A return ticket, please."
"Where to, sir?"
"Back here, please."

(*) Swissair to hang up flying suits

A cafeteria at AAA (Aid for the Ailing Aristocrat); Dr. H. Tessminn (**T**), Fritz von Brausewitz (**B**)[1]:

T: Well, it's a relief to be back in Heidelberg.

B: Where've you been? Was it business?

T: It certainly was business. I had to visit a customer. I had a spell of nine days there. AAA has certainly carved itself a nice niche in the business in Switzerland.

B: How was the flight?

T: It was a bit cramped. But then it usually is.

B: I know what you mean. Charter flights are so crowded that the pilots sometimes go by boat. Or is your large-size frame too big for the seats?

T: No, actually I was referring to the fact that there isn't much space compared with US carriers. Some planes are so small they even have an outside lavatory.

B: Hmmm! How was the catering on board?

T: Much better food than you get on other flights. Best in the world, I'd say.

B: Yes, I read an article recently where they said that Swissair is going to reduce its flying activities and concentrate on offering more value for money in the air and on the ground. It said that the competition was so hard now that there was no more profit to be made with such low fares.

T: So what will happen to the flight operations part of the company? You can't live off food alone.

B: That's the great trick in it all. They want to become a virtual airline. Actually flying passengers only accounted for 40 percent of profit, so it's time for Swissair to hang up its flying suits.

T: It means that we'll probably get a better service when there's a bit more competition around. That's a rule that holds true in general.

B: With aeroplanes around big enough for your oversized person you could fly to your heart's content.

T: And eat till I'm stuffed full. Then I'll need an even bigger plane. By the way, you're not so slim yourself.

---

[1] Meet Fritz von Brausewitz in *Small Talk for Big Business*, rororo 60438

W Word watch

Task 1: Scanning for keywords

Find the words that have almost the same meaning.

provide meals for guests commercially:	*c . . . .*
cost of flight tickets:	*f . . .*
extra quality of services:	*v . . . . services*
a short period of time:	*s . . . .*

Task 2: In other words

Do you remember what they said in the dialogue?

AAA has *found a gap in the market.*	AAA has .... itself a ....
Flying passengers only *make up* 40 % of profit.	Flying passengers only .... 40 % of profit.
It's time for Swissair to *give up flying.*	It's time for Swissair to ....

Task 3: Complete the business idioms: one verb – four phrases

---- {
- up one's flying suits
- on to one's shares
- in the balance
- trophies all over the wall

Time for a smile

Swissair calls itself the most civilised airline.
Under each wing their planes have a deodorant.

Now they are working on a plane that'll seat 450 passengers.
And that's just in the toilet.

P Word power

Task 4: Wordfinder's corner

This exercise will help you to understand the following article.

verb	noun	German
fly	....	Flug
relieve	....	Erleichterung
extend	....	Ausweitung
think	....	Denker
analyse	....	Analytiker

Find words that have almost the same meaning	
find a market gap	....
expand one's activities	.... (one's activities)
a *calm* thinker	a .... thinker
warmed up meals	.... meals
better *profits*	better ....
focus on services	.... on services
be used to warmed up meals	.... to warmed up meals

Task 5: Guesswork

Read the following article without looking at the wordlist. Then come back and guess what the words in *italics* mean.

1. Airlines are beginning *to tire* of flying passengers and cargo around.
   A. müde werden **B.** profitieren **C.** sich spezialisieren
2. Swissair may be the first to become a "*virtual*" airline.
   A. richtige **B.** scheinbare **C.** vielseitige
3. The *balance* came from the company's rapidly expanding airline-related activities.
   A. Gleichgewicht **B.** Rest **C.** Ausgleich
4. It can concentrate on *providing* quality services.
   A. expanding **B.** delivering **C.** offering

Swissair starts to sing for its supper

Airlines are beginning to tire of the messy business of flying passengers and cargo around for little profit. Swissair may be the first to become a 'virtual airline', selling its flight operations so that it can concentrate on providing high value-added services to the airline industry.

Swissair took the first steps towards hanging up its flying suit last year when it reorganised its activities into four sectors under a new name, the SAir Group. Flying passengers and cargo accounted for just half of sales in 1997 and 40 per cent of profits. The balance came from the company's rapidly expanding airline-related activities, notably catering, IT and airport and cargo systems.

The Swiss kitchens cook up the best meals in the skies. Passengers accustomed to receiving reheated swill may be relieved by the rapid extension of Swissair's catering expertise to other carriers. Shareholders may see it as an even better idea. As airline fares continue to fall and smaller carriers struggle to carve a niche, focusing on serving up food and leaving the flying to others offers the prospect of better returns.

Philippe Bruggisser, SAir Group president, plays down a move away from flying, but knows he has created an opportunity to add shareholder value which may be too good to miss. The workaholic Bruggisser arrives at his monastic office at 5am every day and holds management meetings at 5.30. He is known as a quiet thinker and his door is open to employees who arrive with a plan and the numbers to make it work ...

After a spell at Union Bank of Switzerland, Bruggisser became the airline's financial controller before moving to build up the catering and logistics side. 'Everything they are doing with the group structure points to them becoming the world's first virtual airline', says Andrew Barker, airline analyst at SBC Warburg Dillon Read in London.

Doug Cameron, The European, 6–12 April 1998

Digesting the article

Task 6: Did you get the meaning?

Are these statements true (T) or false (F)?

1. Swissair are giving up flying because it is too messy.
2. Catering is more profitable than flying passengers and cargo.
3. In 1997 flying passengers accounted for 50% of the profit.
4. Swissair will cook for other carriers.
5. Bruggisser used to be a financial controller at Union Bank of Switzerland.
6. Airline fares continue to fall.

Task 7: Guided note-taking practice

1. There is little profit in ....
2. There is more profit in ....
3. That is why Swissair ....

Word aid

account for 40 % of profit	40 % des Gewinns ausmachen
airline-related activities	Aktivitäten, die mit Fluggesellschaften zu tun haben
cargo	Fracht
carrier	Fluggesellschaft
carve oneself a niche	sich eine Marktnische schaffen
cater	Speisen und Getränke liefern
competition	Konkurrenz, Wettbewerb
content, to one's heart's ~	nach Herzenslust
cramped	eng, beengt
expand	vergrößern, ausweiten
expertise	Sachkenntnis
extension	Erweiterung, Ausdehnung
fare	Flugpreis
flight	Flug
flight operations	Flüge

focus on	sich konzentrieren auf
frame	hier: Körperbau, Statur
go down to rock bottom	abstürzen (von Preisen)
hang in the balance	auf der Kippe stehen
hang on to one's shares	seine Aktien halten
hang trophies all over the walls	Trophäen an den Wänden aufhängen
hang up one's flying suits	seine Fliegeruniform an den Nagel hängen
meal	Mahlzeit, Gericht
messy	unsauber, unordentlich
monastic office	Büro eines Mönchs
move to build up something	darangehen, etwas aufzubauen
move, a ~ away from	Abkehr von
niche	Nische
notably	besonders, vor allem
offer	anbieten
oversized	zu groß
play down	herunterspielen
prospect of	Aussicht auf
recently	kürzlich, vor kurzem
refer to	hier: meinen, sprechen von
reheat	aufwärmen
relief	Erleichterung, Erlösung
returns	Rendite
sales	Verkäufe, Absatz
seat	Sitz
shareholder	Aktionär
sky	Himmel
slim	schlank
space	Raum, Platz
spell of nine days	Zeitraum von neun Tagen
swill	(Sau-)Fraß
value-added service	verbesserter Service
virtual airline	virtuelle, scheinbare Fluggesellschaft

✔ Boost your reading skills 9: Vertical scanning for meaning

The best speed-readers are able to take in more words *at a glance* than the average reader who can only take in the words that are in a circle of about two centimetres in *diameter.* With some practice that *ability* will develop naturally.

auf einen Blick
Durchmesser
Fähigkeit

Step one

This is an exercise to prepare for the reading skill explained in step two. Take a book, copy a page, *fold* it three or four times (depending on its size) so that the words fall into a series of *rectangles.* Start reading by first looking at the words in the upper left rectangle. Then read those in the *upper right* rectangle; next, move to the words in the second rectangle from the top on the left; and so on down the page. You won't be reading the words in the order in which they're written. But with some practice you'll pick up a great *amount* of information. Being able to take in groups of words out of their normal order is important for the next step.

falten
Rechteck
oberstes rechtes
Menge

Step two

A lot of images and movements come across more clearly when they are viewed *off centre.* Fold a page vertically and follow the *vertical* line with your eyes in a relaxed way.

außerhalb
senkrecht

By allowing images to come in from both sides around your central line of *vision,* you can take in many words and phrases that are off centre from your main *focus* on the page. It's like looking at the centre of a *painting.* Even if you focus your eyes on its middle you are able to take in objects in the *periphery.* And the more words you can *grasp* at a glance, the more quickly you'll move vertically through any text. This what we call scanning for *meaning.* Keep practising.

Gesichtsfeld
Blickzentrum
Gemälde
Rand
erfassen
Bedeutung

Bullying bosses and the Nanny State

OUR STORY: The Nanny State

THE ARTICLE: Bosses face fines for rollicking the workers

Whet your appetite

What with all the unemployment everywhere the representatives of government and industry are always telling us to be more independent. At the same time more rules and regulations are introduced to stop us doing that. The individual becomes less independent. This chapter deals with a lack of common sense and overprotection at the workplace.

Time for a smile

The company has been expanding on the home market. That is why the boss invited his sales team into his office. "You have done so well selling that I'm giving you all a cheque for $1,500," he said, and on second thoughts he added, "... and if you keep on working like this, I might even sign them."

Unbelievable but true: A Spanish bank clerk who received sudden promotion to manager, took revenge on his ex-boss by demoting him to the position of office boy. Among his new tasks, the ex-boss had to copy out the local phone book by hand. Fortunately an industrial tribunal forced the new manager to pay compensation.

(*) The Nanny State

Bryan Hemmung (**B**) is discussing the world of work with Mick Disney (**M**), a former policeman from Nottingham. They are at the job centre.

B: It's a good thing we get this unemployment money as a safeguard. I couldn't live without it.

M: Why don't you try to get a real job? You're workshy. People like you should pay a fine for being out of work too long.

B: Hey, stop bullying me. You're no better, working in Germany and collecting your unemployment money here during your holidays. Actually they should prosecute you.

M: I'm only here a few weeks a year. You pledged to the government that you'd be willing to find or accept a job. There should be a watchdog committee to check upon you and rectify the situation. People have too many rights.

B: So you think all the laws and guidelines should be put on a tighter footing – like in a dictatorship? I can't accept that. Anyway it's not feasible. If you make more laws people will find more ways to get round them.

M: Maybe you're right. Today I read something in the paper that made my blood boil. A worker or employee in a company can take his company to court if he thinks his boss is making too much stress for him.

B: Quite right as well. Some bosses are no more than bullies, pushing their workers around.

M: More than that. Some quango somewhere wants to have rules that both male and female workers should get time off for their sick children. It's crazy.

B: So what you think is that the man should simply stay at his workplace, is it? Oh, look, it's my turn to get my money.

M: Are we going for a pint then?

B: No, mate, no time. I'm doing a bit of private work for a friend.

M: That's typical. Absolutely typical. You're robbing the state.

B: I've got to make ends meet, mate. See you!

Word watch

Task 1: Scanning for keywords

Find the words that have almost the same meaning.

a semi-official committee ....
instructions or directives ....
something that can be done is ... .
push someone around because you're bigger ....

Task 2: In other words

Do you remember how they said it in the dialogue?

You're *not willing to work.*	You're ....
A worker can take *legal action against* his company.	A worker can .... his company ....
Actually, they should *take you to court.*	Actually, they should .... you.
You should pay *money as a penalty.*	You should pay a ....
Rules should *be made stricter.*	.... should be ....

Task 3: Complete the business idioms

Put the verbs in these sentences. Add a preposition where necessary. Be careful to give the correct form of the verb.

put, give, get, take

1. My boss doesn't want to .... me *time off* for my wedding.
2. Workers should be allowed to .... *time off* when their children are sick.
3. But they shouldn't .... *time off* for shopping.
4. Bosses can be .... *court* for .... their employees .... *stress.*
5. The HSE wants to .... rules .... *a tighter footing.*

Word power

Read the article on page 148 first. Then do these exercises.

Task 4: Wordfinder's corner

Find the nouns

prosecute	....	injure	....
feasible	....	employ	....

Find a word that has almost the same meaning as the one in *italics*

bosses must face heavy *penalties*	bosses must face heavy ....
a Government-*financed committee*	a Government-............ ....
unsafe working conditions	....
instructions are *given* to employers	.... are .... to employers
recognise varying degrees of stress	.... varying degrees of stress
calm down unions	.... unions
give someone a rocket	.... a rocket to someone

Find the opposite of the words

legal	....
limited	....
possible	....
loose	....
healthy	....

Time for a smile

"No way!" said the boss. "I cannot give you two hours off for lunch. Think, man, if I did that I would have to do the same for every person whose wife had just had triplets."

An employee went to see his boss. "Excuse me, sir, but I've been working here for over ten years and doing the work of three men. I think it's time I had a raise." – "Well," said the boss, "I must think about giving you a raise, but what about these treee men? Give me their names and I'll fire them!"

Task 5: Words in context

Use the solutions from **task 4** to fill in the gaps in the following sentences.

1. A Code of Practice which puts it on a .... regulatory footing.
2. Bosses who.......... a rocket to workshy staff could end up in court.
3. .... on stress are already .... to employers and employees.
4. It was .... to say what the maximum .... would be.
5. Workers have a legal right to time off if their children are ....
6. Miss Harman's plan will be seen as an attempt to .... unions.

Task 6: Guesswork

Read the following article without looking at the wordlist. Then come back and guess what the words in *italics* mean.

1. A *watchdog* is
A. an executive
B. a security system
C. supervising committee

2. Firms which are found to have caused *injury* ...
A. damages **B.** harm **C.** loss of salary

3. Poor *safeguards* caused injuries
A. protective equipment **B.** technology
C. supervisors

4. A *tighter regulatory footing*
A. stricter rules **B.** more regulations **C.** stricter legal basis

5. It will be seen as an *attempt* to appease the unions.
A. attack **B.** trial **C.** tactic

Bosses face fines for rollicking the workers

Bosses who deliver a rocket to workshy or incompetent staff could end up in court facing heavy fines, it emerged yesterday.

The watchdog Health and Safety Executive revealed it is considering the feasibility of prosecuting employers whose harsh words cause workers to suffer stress.

And in a further symptom of the Nanny State, Social Security Secretary Harriet Harman has let it be known that she is considering giving both male and female workers a legal right to time off if their children are sick.

The HSE, a Government-funded quango, can prosecute companies under the 1974 Health and Safety at Work Act. This requires employers 'to ensure so far as is reasonably practicable' that workplaces are safe.

So far prosecutions, which can result in unlimited fines at crown courts, have involved either cases against firms found to have caused injuries through poor safeguards, or against those who have failed to rectify unsafe conditions after being told to do so by HSE inspectors.

Yesterday a spokesman confirmed: "Guidelines on stress are already issued to employers and employees. But we are currently discussing whether we need a Code of Practice which puts it on a tighter regulatory footing."

She added that there had never yet been a prosecution over stress – and it was therefore impossible to say what the maximum penalty would be.

The HSE was compiling new criteria to help its workplace inspectors to identify varying degrees of stress – and decide whether employers found guilty of causing it should be taken to court, she said.

Recent research has shown that half a million UK employees claim they are suffering stressful pressure at work – either through having to work longer hours to keep their jobs; or bullying bosses treating them badly. Miss Harman's plan to give both fathers and mothers time off to look after sick children will be seen as an attempt to appease unions over workplace rights ...

By David Norris, Daily Mail, 4 May 1998

Digesting the article

Task 7: Did you get the message?

Are these statements true (T) or false (F)?

1. 500,000 employees claim to suffer stress.
2. Guidelines on stress are already in place.
3. Employers can be taken to court if they put workers under unfair stress.
4. Employers have been fined for bullying.

Task 8: Guided note-taking practice

According to the article the HSE ensures three workplace rights:

the right to ....

the right to ....

the right to ....

Word aid

act	hier: Gesetz
appease unions	Gewerkschaften besänftigen
attempt	Versuch
bully	einschüchtern, schikanieren
claim	behaupten
Code of Practice	Verhaltenskodex
collect unemployment money	Arbeitslosengeld abholen
compensation	Schadenersatz
compile criteria	Kriterien sammeln
consider something	etwas in Erwägung ziehen
crown courts	Berufungsgerichte
currently	gegenwärtig
deliver a rocket to someone	jemandem eine Zigarre verpassen
demote someone	degradieren, zurückstufen
emerge	sich zeigen, hervorgehen
employee	Arbeitnehmer

employer	Arbeitgeber
ensure	sicherstellen, gewährleisten
expand	vergrößern
face a fine	mit einer Geldbuße rechnen müssen
fail to do something	versäumen, etwas zu tun
feasibility	Machbarkeit, Durchführbarkeit
feasible	machbar, durchführbar
find guilty	für schuldig befinden
fund an institution	eine Institution finanziell tragen
get along without someone	ohne jemanden auskommen
get round a law	ein Gesetz umgehen
go for a pint	auf ein Bier gehen
guidelines	Richtlinien
harsh words	unsanfte, harte Worte
incompetent staff	unfähige Mitarbeiter
injury	Verletzung
involve cases	Prozesse nach sich ziehen
issue guidelines	Richtlinien herausgeben
job centre	Arbeitsamt
legal right	gesetzliches, legales Recht
let something be known	etwas verkünden
make ends meet	über die Runden kommen
make someone's blood boil	jemanden vor Wut zum Kochen bringen
male and female workers	männliche und weibliche Arbeitnehmer
mate	Kamerad
Nanny State	familiär: Wohlfahrtsstaat
on second thoughts	nach kurzer Überlegung
penalty	Geldstrafe
pressure	Druck
promotion	Beförderung
prosecute	gerichtlich belangen
prosecution	gerichtliche Verfolgung
put a law through	ein Gesetz durchbringen
put something on a tighter footing	etwas auf solidere Grundlage stellen

quango (quasi-autonomous non-government organisation)	halbstaatliche Organisation
reasonably practicable	vernünftig durchführbar
recent	neu, kürzlich
rectify unsafe conditions	unsicheren Arbeitsbedingungen abhelfen
regulatory	Durchführungs-, Ausführungs-
require	verlangen, (er-)fordern
reveal something	enthüllen, eröffnen
rise	Gehaltserhöhung
rollick (informae)	disziplinieren
safeguard	Sicherheitsmaßnahme, Absicherung
sick	krank
social security	Sozialversicherung
staff	Personal
suffer stress	unter Streß leiden
take revenge on	sich rächen an
take time off	Urlaub nehmen
take to court	vor Gericht bringen
treat someone badly	jemanden schlecht behandeln
tribunal	Gericht
UK (United Kingdom)	Vereinigtes Königreich von Großbritannien
unemployment	Arbeitslosigkeit
union	Gewerkschaft
varying degrees of stress	unterschiedliche Grade von Streß
watchdog	Wachhund
workplace rights	Rechte am Arbeitsplatz
workshy	arbeitsscheu

Time for a smile

"Dobson," said the boss one morning, "I just don't know how we are going to get along without you – but starting Monday, we're going to try."

Shop around the clock

OUR STORY: Loosen up a bit!

THE ARTICLE: Welcome to the 24-hour society

Whet your appetite

On the one hand it's good to loosen up all the rules and regulations concerning work. Shops, banks and post offices should stay open in the evenings and at weekends. Customers would be satisfied and turnover would increase. Everybody would be happy. But would they? It appears that ordinary employees are stressed by this irregular life. As with every issue there are pros and cons. You can earn more money, but you have to give something up for it. What would your choice be?

Time for a smile: Shopping

People in Britain are becoming much stronger. Twenty years ago it would take two men to carry £20 worth of supermarket shopping. Now, even a small child can carry it.

I went to the perfume counter in a department store and asked to see and smell some different types of perfume. The assistant asked me: "Is the perfume for your wife, sir – or would you like to see something more expensive?"

(*) Loosen up a bit!

It's Sunday afternoon. Robert Kleinstück (**K**) and Ronald Bossybitch (**B**)[1] are sitting in the office.

K: It's been a damned nuisance correcting this manuscript under time pressure. We were rushed off our feet.

B: Well, it's done now so we can go home and have dinner.

K: I'm sorry, Ronald. I've got nothing at home. I can't accommodate you. We can't buy any food. The shops are closed.

B: It's really hopeless here. Back in England we could go to an off-licence. They're open till midnight.

K: Well, here we prefer our free time. That's our pattern of life. Work, then free time.

B: Have you ever heard of shift-work? You distribute the chores over several people. Then more people have the chance to earn something. And the service is there for the customer.

K: But it's nice to have time off.

B: Of course it is, but you can have time off without closing the whole country down. Employees who work at the weekend can offset their work by getting free days during the week.

K: Not having a fixed life pattern will erode the family. That's what it will lead to. It's not good for the future society.

B: Neither is being unemployed. I predict serious problems if Germany can't become more flexible. I forecast a society of 'haves' and 'have-nots'.

[1] Meet these two characters in *Get Through at Meetings. Business English für Konferenzen und Präsentationen,* rororo 60262.

Word watch

Task 1: Scanning for keywords

Find the words that have almost the same meaning.

making statements about the future	f . . . .
gradually remove or rub away	e . . . .
compensate	o . . . . .
boring, everyday work	c . . . . s

Task 2: In other words

Do you remember how they said it in the dialogue?

That's our *style* of life.	That's our .... of life.
Irregular working hours will *wear* family life *away.*	Irregular working hours will .... family life.
You *spread* the *jobs* over several people.	You .... the .... over several people.
We *had no time for anything.*	We were .... *feet.*

Task 3: Our business idiom: lead

Can you match idiom with meaning?

1	lead to	**A**	be best / first
2	lead the field	**B**	deceive by making false promises
3	lead on	**C**	start
4	lead into	**D**	have as a result
5	lead off with	**E**	guide, show the way to

And now put the above idioms into the correct place

1. Not having a fixed life pattern will erode the family. That's what it will ....
2. The speaker .... with a survey of the company's objectives.
3. Britain is at the start of a social revolution as it .... the world .... becoming a "24-hour society".
4. Microsoft .... in software applications.
5. Some travel agencies .... with their brochures.

Ⓟ Word power

Read the article on page 157 first. Then come back and do these exercises.

Task 4: Wordfinder's corner

Match words from the article with the definitions.

1 list of items to be discussed	**A** pressurise
2 make stress for people	**B** off-licence
3 things to help you to enjoy life	**C** work pattern
4 style, rhythm of work	**D** shift work
5 shop open late for buying food	**E** agenda
6 work irregular hours	**F** entertainment

Find words that have almost the same meaning as those in *italics*.

the report *forecasts* more jobs	the report .... more jobs
employers *put pressure on* workers	employers .... workers
pubs *close* at midnight	pubs .... at midnight
the revolution *gets faster and faster*	the revolution ....
put social *questions* on the agenda	put social ...... on the agenda

Find the opposite of the words in *italics*.

a thing of the *future*	a thing of the ....
numbers *halve* within 10 years	numbers .... within 10 years
feel *relaxed*	feel ....
9*am*	9 ....

Task 5: Words in context

Use your solutions and fill in the gaps in these sentences.

1. People feel even more .... and hectic.
2. Work .... are changing dramatically.
3. Employers are .... workers.
4. More people than ever have part-time or .... contracts.

Task 6: Guesswork

Read the following article without looking at the wordlist. Then come back and guess what the words in *italics* mean.

1. But the advantages are *offset* by the new 'flexible society'.
   A. compensated **B.** eliminated **C.** offered

2. A report *commissioned* from the Future Foundation by BT and First Direct bank is to be published in November.
   A. conducted **B.** composed **C.** ordered

3. It is even possible that schools would have to *consider* opening beyond normal hours into the evening.
   A. think at **B.** think back on **C.** think about

4. People will have to work for varying periods depending on *demand*.
   A. commissions **B.** orders **C.** circumstance

5. The Future Foundation, a new *think-tank* whose declared *aim* is to put social issues on the business agenda.
   A. brains trust **B.** idea **C.** concept
   A. objective **B.** task **C.** strategy

6. Technological innovations like *tele-marketing* are also helping to erode the distinctions between weekend and weekday.
   A. selling by phone **B.** advertising by TV **C.** distance marketing

Time for a smile

In an effort to boost sales, British Airways announced that for two weeks only, any business executive who travelled on a midweek flight could take his wife along with him for only twenty per cent of the normal fare. In order to judge the success of this experiment, they wrote to all the wives concerned, asking them if they had enjoyed their flights. Eighty-five per cent of the wives wrote back asking, "What flight?"

Welcome to the 24-hour society

Britain is leading a social revolution, writes John Vidal

Britain is at the start of a social revolution as it leads the world into becoming a '24-hour society' where people work, shop and play at all times of the day and night.

But the advantages offered by new technologies and the globalisation of business are offset by the new 'flexible society' making people feel even more rushed and hectic.

A report commissioned from the Future Foundation by BT and First Direct bank to be published in November, finds the British work longer hours than anyone else in Europe and that work patterns are changing dramatically. Employers are pressurising workers to work longer hours, and more people than ever have part-time or shift work contracts or work with no fixed hours.

The old 'working day' is becoming a thing of the past, with more than 1 million people working between 9pm and 11pm and at least a third of a million between 2am and 5am. These numbers are forecast to double within 10 years.

The result of the workplace revolution, which is being driven by globalisation and increased market pressures, is pressure on employers, shops and institutions to accommodate people's hectic and time-extended lives.

Already many shops are open until 10pm, pubs shut at midnight, and it is possible to buy books or pizzas or bank in the middle of the night. Doctors, dentists, schools, colleges, town halls and high street shops may all have to follow to adapt to the needs of the more demanding citizen. Taking the flexible society to an extreme, it is even possible that schools would have to consider opening beyond normal hours into the evening.

The report predicts that more jobs will be created as the revolution gathers pace but people will have to work for varying periods depending on circumstance and demand. The Future Foundation, a new think-tank whose declared aim is to put social issues on the business agenda, says the challenge for business is to respond to the new time pressures of people's workhours by opening well beyond 'normal' hours. More than 25 per cent of shoppers are now most likely to shop after 6pm, a 50 per cent increase in a few years.

Increasing numbers view the evening as a time to combine shopping and chores with entertainment and enjoyment, the report found. They want sports services, garages, banks, cinemas, shops, public transport and off-licences to be open beyond their current hours.

Technological innovations like the Internet, tele-marketing, video-conferencing and home banking are also helping to erode the distinctions between night and day and weekend and weekday.

The traditional concepts of when and where to work, play or shop are breaking down with new media and new possibilities of communication with people ...

The Guardian, 24 September 1997

! Digesting the article

Task 7: Scanning for figures

Use the scanning reading skill on page 38 to complete the table.

How many people work between 9pm and 11pm?	.... %
How many people work between 2am and 5am?	.... %
Within how many years will these figures double?	.... %
How many shoppers tend to shop after 6pm?	.... %

Task 8: Did you get the meaning?

What is your opinion? Are you for or against the 24-hour society? Let's weigh the pros and cons as described in the article.

advantages	disadvantages
•	•
•	•
•	•
•	•
•	•
•	•

(V) Word aid

2pm	2 Uhr mittags
9am	9 Uhr vormittags
accomodate	versorgen; sich einstellen, sich anpassen an
advantage	Vorteil
agenda	Tagesordnung
aim	Ziel
appear, it appears	es scheint
bank	Bankgeschäfte tätigen
challenge	Herausforderung
choice	Wahl
chores	Aufgaben, Hausarbeit
circumstances	Verhältnisse, Umstände
close down	schließen, zumachen
commission a report	ein Gutachten in Auftrag geben
conduct	durch-, ausführen, leiten
contract	Vertrag
current hours	hier: normale Geschäftszeiten
customer	Kunde
declared aim	erklärtes Ziel
demand	Nachfrage
demanding citizens	anspruchsvolle Bürger
department store	Kaufhaus
depend on	abhängen von
distinction	Unterschied
distribute	verteilen
employer	Arbeitgeber
erode the family	das Familienleben aushöhlen
expensive	teuer
fixed hours	feste Arbeitszeiten
forecast	vorhersagen
gather pace	Geschwindigkeit aufnehmen
have time off	Freizeit haben
haves and have-nots	Reiche und Arme
increase	steigen, wachsen, steigern

issue	Frage, Problem
loosen	lockern
nuisance, it's a ~	es ist ärgerlich
objective	Ziel
off-licence	(Schank-)Konzession
offset	kompensieren, ausgleichen
part-time work	Halbtagsarbeit
past	Vergangenheit
pattern of life	Lebensstil, Lebensrhythmus
predict	voraussagen
pressure	Druck
pressurise	Druck ausüben auf
pros and cons	Für und Wider
publish	veröffentlichen
regulations	Vorschriften
respond	reagieren, Antwort finden
rush, be rushed off one's feet	unter Zeitdruck stehen
rushed	gehetzt
rushed, feel ~	sich gehetzt fühlen
shift-work	Schichtarbeit
shop	einkaufen
social issues	soziale Fragen
start; be at the ~ of a revolution	vor einer Revolution stehen
stay open	geöffnet bleiben
take to an extreme	auf die Spitze treiben
think-tank	Denkfabrik
turnover	Umsatz
unemployed	arbeitslos
varying periods	unterschiedliche Zeiten
weigh the pros and cons	das Für und Wider abwägen
work patterns	Arbeitsweise, Arbeitsrhythmus

Making both ends meet

OUR STORY: Black work or no work

THE ARTICLE: Why millions are moonlighting to make ends meet

Whet your appetite

It's easy to point a finger at all the "black work" that is going on all over Europe. It takes jobs away from the honest citizens and it increases unemployment. But before we identify another "black sheep" in our midst, we should think about why it's happening. Doesn't the cost of living always rise to exceed income? And aren't the overall costs of work, the burden of tax and social contributions too high? Employers are afraid to take on new workers. So some people can't get work. What would you do in that situation?

Time for a smile

A young man who was just about to embark on a business career went to see his grandfather, who had founded the family firm.
"Remember, my boy, that in business honesty is still the best policy."
"Right, grandfather," said the grandson.
"But before you do anything else, read up on company law," recommended the old man. "You'd be surprised at the kind of things you can do in the name of business and still be honest."

(*) Black work or no work

Robert Kleinschroth (**K**) and René Bosewitz (**B**) are sitting in the sauna of their training club, the Unsporty Garden.

K: I'm really fed up with Sabrina and her Unsporty Garden. This renovation work has been going on too long. It's three months already. I pay DM 90 per month for this. I can hardly make ends meet at home, money is so short. Sabrina is exploiting us.

B: Oh, I guess she expects us to turn a blind eye to all this trouble.

K: Well, they should create some legislation against this sort of thing.

B: Sabrina is an entrepreneur. She can allow herself everything.

K: Yes, I'm sure these workers here are not in a trade union. She'll be paying them as little as possible. Damn, now the sauna oven has switched itself off. It's getting cold in here.

B: That's probably better anyway.

K: What do you mean? You know, René, I've told you before the important thing is not the heat but the temperature difference. That's why the cold shower is so important.

B: Thanks for the lecture, Robert, but there won't be any temperature difference today.

K: Why not?

B: Because there isn't any cold water. There's nothing coming out of the shower.

K: My god, I'm going to cancel my contract. Why don't those workers finish their work? I'd fire them immediately.

B: No, you wouldn't because they're not employed.

K: What are they doing here if they're not employed?

B: Robert, are you walking around with your eyes shut? They're moonlighting.

K: Moonlighting?

B: Yes, they're working without paying tax or social contributions.

K: You mean they're not legal, not legitimate?

B: Yes, Robert, this little workforce is working in the shadow economy. They cost the countries of Europe billions.

K: Well, I'm going to reduce my monthly membership fee immediately. You know that's absolutely typical of Sabrina. And I'm beginning to see the light. That explains why none of them replied to me when I asked them some questions.

B: Right, Robert, they can't speak German.

Word watch

Task 1: Scanning for keywords

Find the words in the dialogue that have almost the same meaning.

written agreement between two parties	*c . . . . . . t*
work in the black economy	*m . . . .*
something that is legal	*l . . . . e*
total number of employees in a company	*w . . . . e*
organisation of workers	*t . . . . u . . . .*

Task 2: In other words

Do you remember the way it was said in the dialogue?

She expects us *not to see.*	She expects us ....
These workers here *are not organised.*	These workers here are not ....
I can hardly *live on my salary.*	I can hardly ....
They should *make* some *laws* against this sort of thing.	They should create some .... against this sort of thing.
Sabrina is *taking advantage of* us.	Sabrina is .... us.
She is a *businesswoman.*	She is an ....

Task 3: Complete the business idioms: One verb – five idioms

---- {
- a blind eye
- over 5 million a year
- over a new leaf
- up the pressure
- something upside down

Ⓟ Word power

Task 4: Wordfinder's corner

Match words from the article on page 166 with the translations.

Find a word that has a similar meaning

1	van	**A**	Fabrik
2	plant	**B**	Sozialabgaben
3	social security	**C**	Sozialversicherung
4	social deductions	**D**	Lieferwagen
5	income tax	**E**	Anzeichen
6	indications	**F**	Einkommensteuer

Find the verb

legislation	....	Gesetze
exploitation	....	ausbeuten
contribution	....	beitragen
security	....	sichern

Task 5: Words in context

Put the solutions to *task 4* into the sentences in their correct forms.

1. They pick up workers in (*Lieferwagen*) and take them off to farms and factories.
2. Nobody pays any (*Steuer*) or (*Sozialversicherung*).
3. It is common to find young girls working in textile (*Fabriken*).
4. Families know they are being (*ausgebeutet*), but claim it's better than not working.
5. The company saves on (*Sozialbeiträge*) and the worker saves on (*Einkommensteuer*).

Task 6: Guesswork

Read the article on page 166. Then come back and guess the meaning of the words in *italics*.

1. Every morning in *remote* villages *corporals* can be seen waiting on street corners.
   A. entlegen B. groß C. stadtnah
   A. Korporal B. Carabinieri C. Vorarbeiter

2. *Conditions are cramped* and dirty and the girls earn less than L10,000 a day.
   A. Bedingungen sind hart
   B. Lebensverhältnisse sind bescheiden
   C. Arbeitsplatzverhältnisse sind beengt

3. *According* to first indications, social duties would be calculated on 25 per cent of the wages handed over in cash.
   A. In Anbetracht B. Nach C. Voraussichtlich

4. Across Europe the shadow labour market accounts for up to 16 per cent of *GDP*.
   A. Bruttosozialprodukt
   B. Nettoeinkommen pro Kopf
   C. Gesamte Devisen-Planung

Time for a smile

The young man was desperate for money and so on his holidays he decided to take a job in a local factory. "Now," said the foreman, "your first job is to sweep the floor."
"But I've got a BA degree," said the young man, "and I'm currently studying for a masters in business administration."
"Oh," said the foreman. "In that case I'd better show you how to hold the broom."

Why millions are moonlighting to make ends meet

Every morning in remote villages in southern Italy corporals can be seen waiting on street corners. These corporals control an underground workforce. They pick up workers in vans and take them off to farms and factories for a day's work. They pay them in cash on the way home, having taken out their own commission. Nobody pays any tax or social security. The authorities know what is going on but turn a blind eye to the practice.

Elsewhere in the south, it is common to find young girls, some as young as 10, working in textile plants. Conditions are cramped and dirty and the girls earn less than L10,000 ($5) a day. Families know they are being exploited but claim it's better than not working.

"Sometimes illegal workers can get more money than their regular colleagues," says Mario Sai, director of the department for the south at CGIL, Italy's biggest trade union. "Around Naples, for example, small firms specialising in luxury goods pay their workers a bonus for not having a contract. The company saves on social contributions and the worker saves on income tax."

The Italian government is planning new legislation to allow companies to become legitimate without fear of being punished for their past activities. Entrepreneurs would be asked to start paying regular taxes and contributions, with an amnesty for their dishonest past. According to first indications, previous social deductions would be calculated on 25 per cent of the wages handed over in cash. Across Europe the shadow labour market accounts for up to 16 per cent of GDP.

Marc Champion and Michele Puccioni,
The European, 6–12 April 1998

Time for a smile

Doesn't it make you feel a little insecure to know that if you're a human being, your body is worth 98 cents – and if you're a cow, it's worth $700?

Digesting the article

Task 7: Scanning for facts and figures

1. How old are the youngest textile workers? __ years
2. How much do they earn a day? $ __
3. How many percent of the European GDP does the shadow labour market account for? __ %

Task 8: Scanning for key phrases

You've read the article. Find the key sentence for each paragraph.

Paragraph 1: ....

Paragraph 2: ....

Paragraph 3: ....

Paragraph 4: ....

Word aid

about, be ~ to do something	sich daranmachen, etwas zu tun
account for	sich belaufen auf, ausmachen
amnesty	Amnestie
authorities	Behörden
BA (bachelor)	akademischer Grad
broom	Besen
business administration	Betriebswirtschaft
cancel a contract	einen Vertrag kündigen
claim	behaupten; beanspruchen
cold dip	Tauchbecken
commission	Provision
contract	Vertrag
contributions	Beiträge
corporal	hier: Vorarbeiter
cramped conditions	beengte Arbeitsplatzverhältnisse
deductions	Steuern, Abgaben

desperate, be ~ for money	in verzweifelter Geldnot sein
dishonest	unehrlich
embark on a career	eine Karriere beginnen
employed	angestellt
entrepreneur	Unternehmer
exploit	ausbeuten
fed, be ~ up with	die Nase voll haben von
GDP, Gross Domestic Product	Bruttosozialprodukt
honesty	Ehrlichkeit
indications	Anzeichen
insecure	unsicher
legislation	Gesetz, Gesetzgebung
legitimate	rechtmäßig, legitim
make ends meet	über die Runden kommen
membership fee	Mitgliedsbeitrag
moonlight	schwarzarbeiten
plant	Fabrik
previous	vorausgehend, früher
remote villages	entlegene Dörfer
shadow labour market	schwarzer Arbeitsmarkt
social contributions	Sozialbeiträge
social security	Sozialversicherung
sweep the floor	den Boden fegen
switch off	ausschalten
trade union	Gewerkschaft
turn a blind eye	ein Auge zudrücken
underground workforce	Arbeiterschaft im Untergrund
van	Lieferwagen
wage	Lohn

Telebusiness from Ireland

OUR STORY: The boom called Ireland

THE ARTICLE: This is Ireland calling

Whet your appetite

The European Union has brought about many changes and many chances. The weaker economies have been supported financially to give them a boost. Ireland is an example of a country that has seized the opportunity with both hands. While keeping their old traditions they have at the same time shown that there is a life beyond oysters and Guinness today.

Time for a smile

Never simply say, "Sorry, we don't have what you are looking for." Always say, "Too bad, I just sold the last one today."
Robert Skole

The demand is greatest for the item that is just out of stock.

Any fool can paint a picture, but it takes a wise man to be able to sell it.
Samuel Butler

(*) The boom called Ireland

Tom Shanahan (T) and Ron Bossybitch (**R**) are eating fish and chips together at O'Reilly's Irish Pub in Heidelberg.

R: This fish'n chips is incredibly good. It reminds me of home.

T: By home you mean England, I suppose. Well, as an Irishman I have to tell you that fish'n chips and the English language are two of the few things we have in common.

R: So you're missing the old country then. When and where are you going back to?

T: I'm a graduate of University College, Dublin, so I'll go to the capital. Of course, the city's changed a bit in the last years. It's a sprawling metropolis nowadays.

R: Yes, you've got a real boom in Ireland. Your economy is even outstripping the British economy, isn't it?

T: It sure is. We saw a chance to get a foot in the door with this European Union. Now we've got a great chance to do business with the Europeans. Not just with Great Britain.

R: When are you going back to Dublin, then?

T: For the summer period. I'm going to work in telebusiness. I'll work at a switchboard and answer queries from all over Europe. Suppliers and customers from European countries phone in toll-free. It doesn't cost them a penny. And I give them information.

R: Good idea! I read a survey which showed that about 70 percent of customers are happy to buy and sell over the phone. What's the pay like?

T: Oh, it's not so good but that doesn't matter. I'll be back at the centre of things for a while. I know I'd earn more in the manufacturing sector, but I can practise my German, too.

Word watch

Task 1: Scanning for keywords

Find the words that have almost the same meaning.

business by phone	t . . . .
advertising and selling by phone	t . . . .
market study	market . . . . . .
phone-call free of charge	t . . . . call

Task 2: In other words

Do you remember how they said it in the dialogue?

This fish'n chips is *unbelievably* good.	This fish'n chips is .... good.
I *got my degree from* University College.	I'm a .... of University College.
Your economy is even *growing faster than* the British economy.	Your economy is even .... the British economy.
It's a *rapidly growing* metropolis.	It's a .... metropolis.

Task 3: Complete the business idioms

Put the verbs into the dialogue. Mind the tenses.

come, do, get, make, set, have

Ron: I was in Ireland last week trying to .... up a language school. I .... a call to a real estate agent to check on prices for a building.

Tom: I think you might have .... a foot in the door three years ago. With the boom in Ireland rents don't .... as cheap as they used to do.

Ron: Yes, the high cost of living is something you .... in common with Germany.

Tom: Well, I guess you'll have to invest a lot if you want to .... business in Ireland.

Ⓟ Word power

Read the article first. Then come back and do these exercises.

Task 4: Wordfinder's corner

Find a word that has almost the same meaning as the words in *italics*.

money to motivate the workforce	....
answer a *question*	answer a .....
make a call *free of charge*	make a .... call
show someone's language skills	.... someone's language skills
exceed the demand of linguists	.... the demand of linguists
a cultural *change*	a cultural ....
watch the market carefully	.... the market carefully
the market is less *developed*	the market is less ....
having to use the telephone	.... to use the telephone
create call centres	.... call centres

Task 5: Words in context

Use the solutions from *task 4* and fill in the gaps.

1. Before you launch a new product you must .... the market.
2. A low salary is no .... for workers to do their best.
3. The European Union has .... very slowly.
4. Multilingual graduates answer .... and take orders from all over Europe.
5. Flags .... his or her language skills.

Time for a smile

A market analyst is a person who tells you what is going to happen within six months and then after that tells you why it didn't.

Task 6: Guesswork

Read the following article without looking at the wordlist. Then come back and guess what the words in *italics* mean.

1. They say it *translates* into $275bn worth of goods.
A. interprets **B.** converts **C.** represents

2. There are certain unemployment *blackspots* in Europe.
A. statistics **B.** negative figures **C.** bad regions

3. They enjoy generous *start-up incentives.*
A. finanzielle Anreize zur Firmengründung
B. erhöhte finanzielle Anfangsanreize
C. schnelle finanzielle Anfangsanreize

4. The *principle reason* for the Irish call centre phenomenon is the fact that they come very cheap.
A. der prinzipielle Grund
B. das Grundprinzip
C. der hauptsächliche Grund

! This is Ireland calling

As the telephone has become an integral part of our daily lives, demand for call centres is booming. Some 20 % of Europe's call centres are now based in Ireland, enjoying the benefits of a willing workforce and generous start-up incentives.

A German who wants United Parcel Service to deliver a document from Berlin to Frankfurt and a Spaniard with a query about Windows 95 have one thing in common: they must both make a toll-free call to Ireland.

The most likely recipient of that call will be a young Irish graduate sitting at a desk with a German, French or Italian flag, indicating his or her language skills. Call centres range from relatively small operations; others such as the sprawling Gateway 2000 C near Dublin airport, have scores of multilingual workers taking orders for computers from Hamburg to Lisbon. With demand for linguists outstripping demand, call centres are hiring more native speakers.

Part of a cultural shift that is taking place across Europe, the fact is that the Europeans are getting used to, or rather are increasingly being obliged to use the telephone to organise their lives. Indeed, recent surveys show that 70 % of UK customers are happy to do business over the phone. Telecoms suppliers and inward investment agencies are well aware of the fact.

Imported from the USA, where telebusiness has long been accepted as the norm, the majority of Irish call centres are the result of American inward investment, looking to get a foot in the door of European markets at a reasonable cost.

The lessons from the US market are clear: 67 million Americans buy something over the phone every year. The US Direct Marketing Association says that translates into $275bn worth of goods and an incredible four million jobs.

In Europe, the market is less evolved, but growing rapidly. By 2000, research suggests that a fifth of Europe's $33bn direct marketing turnover could be conducted through call centres.

As Margaret Molloy, the vice president of marketing at Telecom Eireann, comments: "There are 400 million consumers in Europe. Companies such as Gateway 2000, Best Western, Digital and Dell have all set up pan-European call centres in Ireland as a way to differentiate their services."

Some 20 % of Europe's call centres are now located in Ireland. A further 30 % of all new business is also going to Ireland says the Irish Industrial Development Agency.

The principle reason for the Irish call centre phenomenon, other than the steady stream of multilingual graduates, is the fact that they also come very cheap. But there is more to it than Ireland's unemployment troubles – there are, after all far worse unemployment blackspots in Europe – most notably the cheapest telecoms infrastructure for international calls in Europe. Telemarketing and sales salaries are, however, low and are generally lower than for manufacturing industries ....

Business Age Magazine, No. 77, May 1998

Digesting the article

Task 7: Scanning for figures

Ireland and the United Kingdom

European call centres now based In Ireland ...... %
New call centres going to Ireland ...... %
UK customers doing business on the phone ...... %

Direct marketing in the USA

Americans buying over the phone every year $........................
Jobs secured by call centres $........................
Goods sold over the phone every year $........................

Task 8: Guided note-taking practice

Why are there so many call centres in Ireland?

1. ....
2. ....
3. ....
4. ....

Word aid

accept as a norm	als Norm akzeptieren
be aware of a fact	sich einer Tatsache bewußt sein
be obliged to do	gezwungen sein, zu tun
benefit	Vorteil, Nutzen, Gewinn
conduct	abwickeln, durchführen, leiten
consumer	Konsument
cultural shift	kultureller Wandel, Verlagerung
demand	Nachfrage
dial a wrong number	eine falsche Nummer wählen
differentiate	hier: spezialisieren
enjoy the benefits of	die Vorzüge von ... genießen

evolve a market	einen Markt entwickeln
facilities	Einrichtungen, Anlagen
flag	Flagge
flick on and off	ein- und ausschalten
further 30%	weitere 30%
generous	großzügig
get a foot in the door	einen Fuß in die Tür bekommen
get used to	sich gewöhnen an
graduate	Absolvent
have something in common	etwas gemeinsam haben
incentives	Leistungsanreize, Leistungsprämien
increasingly	zunehmend
incredible	unglaublich
indicate	anzeigen, andeuten
inward investment agency	Investmentagentur, die im Ausland investiert
joy	Freude
language skills	Sprachkenntnisse
light switch	Lichtschalter
linguist	Sprachwissenschaftler
market analyst	Marktanalytiker
multilingual	vielsprachig
order	Auftrag
outstrip	übertreffen, überrunden
pan-European	europaweit
query	Anfrage, Rückfrage
range from ... to	sich von ... bis erstrecken, variieren
reasonable	vernünftig
recent	jüngste, kürzlich, neu
recipient of the call	der Empfänger des Gesprächs
research	Forschung
scores	hier: Dutzende
set up	einrichten, aufbauen
sprawl	sich ausbreiten
start-up incentives	finanzielle Anreize zur Firmengründung

steady stream	ständiger (Zu-)Strom
stock, run out of ~	nicht mehr auf Lager haben
suggest	nahelegen, vorschlagen
supplier	Lieferant
supply	Lieferung
survey	Studie, Umfrage
take orders	Aufträge annehmen
take place	stattfinden
telebusiness	Telefongeschäfte
toll-free call	gebührenfreies Gespräch
translate into $75bn	75 Milliarden Dollar bedeuten
turnover	Umsatz
unemployment blackspots	Gegenden mit hoher Arbeitslosigkeit
willing workforce	arbeitswillige Arbeiterschaft

Time for a smile: The joy of telephoning

In my house there's this light switch that doesn't do anything.
Every so often I would flick it on and off just to check.
Yesterday, I got a call from a woman in Germany. She said, "Stop it."

Today I dialled a wrong number. The other person said, "Hello?"
and I said, "Hello, could I speak to Joey?"...
He said, "Ugh ... I don't think so ... he's only two months old."
I said, "I'll wait."

Between bulls and bears

OUR STORY: Innocents on the stockmarket
THE ARTICLE: Ten points to consider when investing in the stockmarket

Whet your appetite

A few years ago if you had money, you put it in a deposit account and waited for your savings to pile up. Nowadays the interest is so low that you have to do something else with your money. Off to the Stock Exchange! But what to buy? Here's some advice.

Time for a smile

Stockbroker at the hospital: "Tell me, nurse, what is my temperature?"
Nurse: "A hundred and one."
Stockbroker: "When it gets to a hundred and two – sell."

Recession: When you lose your job.
Depression: When I lose my job.

⊛ Innocents on the stockmarket

Bob (**B**) and Ron (**R**) are discussing financial matters.

B: Are you a bull or a bear, Ron?

R: Neither. I'm a decent human being and an honest taxpayer and I don't trust the stockmarket any more. You see, Bob, I invested a lot of money with a stockbroker and got no return on investment. I made heavy losses.

B: You should get to know my stockbroker. I call him Mark. That's short for Marquis de Sade.

R: Well, brokers will be brokers, but that company called Azimeria in Düsseldorf swindled me.

B: Swindled? What did they do? Made wrong predictions for you?

R: That'd be no problem. I told them "no investment in options". It's too dangerous. But they did it anyway. I paid in a lump sum of DM 60,000 and they lost everything.

B: You'd have been better off spreading the risk. Variety ensures safety. You have to be careful with buying and selling on the stockmarket. Don't just buy! You have to check if the company is sound. Especially with a one-off investment.

R: Nowadays I put my money in the building society where I've got a deposit account. It's the best sort of savings scheme.

B: But you don't get more interest than the inflation rate. Listen, for all sorts of information about funds and performers etc., don't waste time talking to me. Seek the advice of a professional, or better still, read the business press regularly. Look here, I happen to have a most interesting article with me. It shows you what to consider when investing in the stockmarket.

Word watch

Task 1: Scanning for keywords

Find the words that have almost the same meaning.

spend money to make a profit	*i* . . . . .
statement about the future	*p* . . . .
quantity of money given in a single payment	*l* . . . . . .
where the bank keeps your money	*d* . . . .
healthy and likely to produce the right result	*s* . . . .

Task 2: In other words

Do you remember how they said it in the dialogue?

I *made no profit* on my investment.	I got no .... on investment.
You'd have been better off *investing in various things to reduce* the risk.	You'd have been better off .... the risk.
Variety *guarantees* safety.	Variety .... safety.

Task 3: Complete the business idioms

Put the verbs into the dialogue.
Add prepositions if necessary and mind the tenses.

seek: suchen **spread: ausbreiten, verteilen**

1. The strike is .... other companies.
2. The meeting has brought the results we were all ....
3. We're always .... improve productivity.
4. We should .... our risks. Variety for safety.
5. We will have to .... the cost over the year.

Ⓟ Word power

Task 4: Wordfinder's corner

Match the English terms with their German equivalents.

A	unit trust (plan)	**1**	Sparplan
B	investment trust	**2**	Erfolgsaktie
C	tracker fund	**3**	einmalige Investition
D	Pep allowances	**4**	Sparzuschüsse vom Finanzamt
E	one-off investment	**5**	Aktienindex-Fonds
F	performer	**6**	Investmentgesellschaft
G	savings scheme	**7**	Kapitalanlagevertrag

Task 5: Words in context

Scan through the headlines of the article on page 183 and find the words that fit the expressions in *italics*.

Which fund to *choose*?	Which fund to ....?
Don't go abroad.	....
What about a *fund that follows an index*?	What about *a* ....?
Should you invest through a *savings scheme with tax relief*?	Should you invest through a ....?
Don't *get nervous.*	Don't ....
A strong desire for money is dangerous.	.... is dangerous.
Take your time.	....

Time for a smile

Customer: "I'd have to be an idiot to buy stock in your company."
Director: "Well, how many shares do you want?"

Are stockbrokers so called because they sell stock that makes you broke?

Task 6: Guesswork

Read the following article without looking at the wordlist. Then come back and guess what the words in *italics* mean.

1. Are you *convinced* that the stockmarket is the right place for your money?
   A. überzeugt B. unsicher C. überrascht

2. Are you *confident* about picking the best companies?
   A. erfahren B. unsicher C. sicher

3. Look for a fund with a *consistent performance record* over three years.
   A. beständige Gewinnbilanz
   B. zuverlässige Perfomanzrekorde
   C. konstantes Spitzenpapier

4. Don't *dabble* in overseas markets if you are not confident.
   A. investieren B. sich einlassen auf C. spekulieren

5. *Drip-feeding* your money in the stockmarket can be safer than making a *one-off investment.*
   A. absichern A. einmalige Investition
   B. reinvestieren B. alles auf eine Karte setzen
   C. in Raten investieren C. Investmentsparen

6. The UK stockmarket won't always produce returns *in excess of* 20 % a year.
   A. in etwa von B. von mehr als C. im Schnitt von

7. Ignore the *scaremongering* in the financial pages of the national press.
   A. Ratschläge B. Versprechungen C. Panikmache

Ten points to consider when investing in the stockmarket

If you are convinced by your arguments that the UK stockmarket is the right place for you to be investing over the next 10 years, then what should you do next?

1. How to invest

If you are not confident about picking the best companies or predicting the right sectors, invest in either a unit trust or investment trust to spread the risk. Seek the advice of a professional; it is worth paying for whether you are investing £25 a month or £25,000 because you are making an important decision.

2. Which fund to pick

Look for a fund with a consistent performance record over at least three years. The top performers over a year have often achieved their position by luck or one clever investment. The best performers over a long period have produced the results through skill and by not taking too many risks. Remember: you are investing for the long term – five years or more.

3. How to spread the risk

If you already have a unit trust or investment trust with one group, think about investing with a different group to spread risk. It is unlikely – unless you are very unlucky – that both groups will perform badly at the same time.

4. Variety provides safety

Spread risk by investing in funds or groups with different styles or specialities. For example, if you have some money with a fund which invests in large companies, invest a bit extra in a fund which specialises in smaller companies. So if one sector struggles, the other fund will probably do better.

5. What about a tracker?

Balance your investments by combining a tracker fund – designed to follow an index – with an active fund whose manager tries to pick the best shares on the stockmarket. If the index does not move up fast, then the active manager may produce better returns.

6. Stay at home

Don't dabble in overseas markets if you are not confident. Don't get sucked in by clever marketing about investment fashions unless you understand what they really mean.

7. Should you invest through a Pep?

Use as much of your Pep allowances as you can afford before 5 April next year. If you cannot put in a lump sum, start a regular savings scheme. You will not miss £25 or £50 a month, and drip feeding your money into the stockmarket can be easier than trying to guess exactly the right time to make a one-off investment.

8. Greed is dangerous

Don't be greedy. The UK stockmarket won't always produce returns in excess of 20 % a year, but as long as it comfortably beats the average bank or building society savings account – currently at 4 % net on average for 90-day deposit accounts and just 2.72 % net on the average instant access account – and inflation, currently 3.4 %, your savings are growing at a real rate.

9. Don't panic

If there is a stockmarket correction, don't panic. Do what the professionals do – if you do have spare money, invest it in the stockmarket as good companies and funds will be cheaper.

10. Be patient

Remember: this is a long-term investment. Ignore the day-to-day news and the scaremongering in the financial pages of the national press and just keep an eye on the important issues: inflation and economic growth. As long as they are sound, the economy will be too – and the stockmarket will produce decent returns on your investment.

Digesting the article

Task 7: Fishing for facts

Are the following statements from the text true(T) or false (F)?

1. If there is a correction of the stockmarket you should sell immediately.
2. It is important to invest a lump sum in a Pep scheme.
3. A tracker fund selects the best shares on the market.
4. If you aren't sure where to invest, pay into an investment fund.

Task 8: Did you get the meaning?

1. The author thinks the investor should
   - A. put his money into a safe stock.
   - B. put his money into various stocks and funds.
   - C. look for a fund with a consistent performance over one year.

2. He is of the opinion you should invest at home because
   - A. inflation is high abroad.
   - B. it's sometimes difficult to understand what's going on abroad.
   - C. foreign marketing is not trustworthy.

3. You needn't panic when there is a correction of the market because you
   - A. have invested through a Pep.
   - B. have made a long-term investment.
   - C. have invested at home.

Ⓥ Word aid

achieve a position	eine Position erreichen
broke	pleite, bankrott
confident	überzeugt, zuversichtlich
consistent	beständig, stetig
convince	überzeugen
currently	zur Zeit
dabble	herumspielen mit, Liebhaberei betreiben
decent returns	gute Gewinne
deposit account	Sparkonto
drip feed money into a fund	Geld nach und nach in einem Fonds anlegen
greed	Gier
innocent (adj, n)	unschuldig, Unschuldige(r)
instant access account	Girokonto
interest	Zins
investment trust	Investmentgesellschaft
issue	Frage, Problem
long term	langfristig
one-off investment	einmalige Investition
patient	geduldig
Pep allowances	steuerbegünstigtes Sparen
performance	Leistung
performer	hier: Erfolgsaktie
pick the best	das Beste herauspicken
predict	vorhersagen
put in a lump sum	einen großen Betrag auf einmal anlegen
record	Vergangenheit, Ruf
return	Rendite, Gewinn
savings account	Sparkonto
savings scheme	Sparplan
scaremongering	Panikmache
seek advice	Rat suchen

seek a solution	nach einer Lösung suchen
share	Aktie
skill	Geschick, Fertigkeit
sound	gesund
spread costs over the year	Kosten übers Jahr verteilen
spread risks	Risiken verteilen
spread to	sich ausbreiten auf
stock	Aktien
stockbroker	Börsenmakler
stockmarket correction	Korrektur der Kurswerte
struggle	kämpfen
suck in	aufsaugen, verschlingen
tax relief	Steuererleichterung, hier: steuerliche Förderung
tracker fund	Fonds, der in Werten des Aktienindex anlegt
unit trust (plan)	Kapitalanlagevertrag
variety	Abwechslung, Vielfalt

✔ Boost your reading skills 10: Reading and mind-mapping

Most people read and forget what they have read. What's the best way to remember an important article? Make a mind-map.

Get an *overview*

Überblick

Understand the structure of what you read. Look the entire article over quickly. Are there *maps*, diagrams or pictures? Does the author use *subtitles*? If so, they are useful *guides* through the text. Ask yourself what exactly you want to learn from the text.

Karten
Untertitel
Führer

Read and take notes in the *margin*

Rand

As you read, you should make light marks in the margin with a pencil, but don't underline the text. The marks may be simple *arrows, key-words*, symbols or questions.

Pfeil, Schlüsselwort

You can take a key-word from the text, but a word that you choose yourself and which *summarises* a paragraph is better.

zusammenfassen

Create a mind-map from your key-words

A mind-map is visual. Here are some *rules* for a mind-map.

Regeln

- ❒ A *coloured* image in the centre. — *farbig*
- ❒ Main ideas *branch off* the centre. — *abzweigen*
- ❒ *Main ideas* should be in larger letters than secondary ideas. — *Hauptgedanken*
- ❒ Always one word per line.
- ❒ Words should always be *printed.* — *in Druckbuchstaben*
- ❒ Lines should be *connected.* This helps your memory to associate. The connected lines should be the same *length* as the word. — *zusammenhängen*; *Länge*
- ❒ Use as many images as possible. It helps your memory and your understanding.

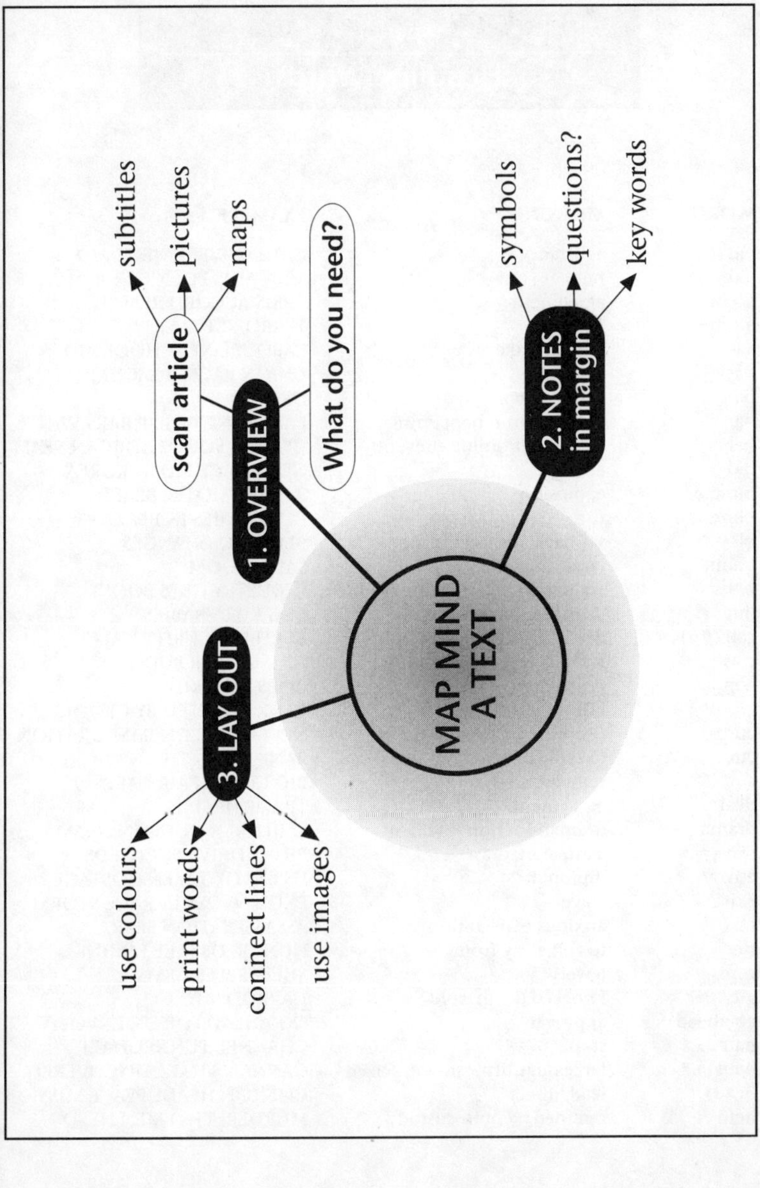
MAP MIND A TEXT
1. OVERVIEW
scan article
subtitles
pictures
maps
What do you need?
2. NOTES in margin
symbols
questions?
key words
3. LAY OUT
use colours
print words
connect lines
use images

Appendix A
Headline Words

WORD	MEANING	EXAMPLE
aid	assistance	£10M GOVERNMENT AID
aid	help	MAN AIDS POLICE
accord	agreement	ARMS ACCORD REACHED
alert	warning	TERRORIST ALERT
axe	destroy, take away	LABOUR AXE SCHOOL AID
back	support	UNION BACKS PEACE MOVE
ban	prohibition	DRUG BAN
bar	prevent from happening	LAST-MINUTE SLIP BARS WIN
bar	exclude, prohibit, prevent	UK BARS SOUTH AFRICAN TEAM
bid	attempt	NEW PEACE BID IN KOREA
blast	explosion	3 DIE IN HOTEL BLAST
blaze	fire	FAMILY DIES IN BLAZE
blow	set-back, disappointment	BLOW TO CHANGES
boom	large increase	SALES BOOM
boost	sudden increase, help, incentive	INDUSTRY GETS BOOST
bug	disease infection, virus	BUG KILLS BABIES
call (for)	demand	BETTER SECURITY CALL
clash	violent argument, conflict	CLASH OVER BUDGET
cop	policeman	COPS SAVE KIDS
crook	criminal	BANK CHEATED BY CROOK
curb	restraint, restriction, limit	NEW CURBS ON IMMIGRATION
cut	to reduce, lower	BANK RATE CUT
cut	reduction	BIG CUTS IN AIR FARES
deal	agreement	TRADE DEAL
drama	dramatic action, incident	CHILDREN IN TRAIN DRAMA
drive	campaign, effort	PEACE DRIVE SUCCEEDS
envoy	diplomat	US ENVOY TAKEN HOSTAGE
exit	leave	EXIT ENVOYS IN RACE STORM
fear	anxious expectation	ASSASSINATION FEAR
flee	to run away from	HUNDREDS FLEE FAMINE
gems	jewels	SHEIK SELLS GEMS
go	knocked down, sold	HARROD'S TO GO
go-ahead	approval	GO-AHEAD FOR UN ENVOY
halt	stop	CHANNEL TUNNEL HALT
haul	large quantity – stolen, seized	CANNABIS HAUL DISCOVERED
head	lead, direct	CLINTON HEADS PEACE MISSION
held	retained, kept in custody	MURDER: TWO MEN HELD

hit	affect badly	SNOW HITS OLYMPICS IN JAPAN
hold	detain in police custody	SUSPECTS HELD
horror	horrifying incident	PLANE HORROR
hurdle	obstacle	NEW HURDLE TO PEACE
jail	to imprison	KILLER JAILED
jobless	unemployed	NUMBER OF JOBLESS INCREASES
key	essential, vital	KEY WITNESS DIES
kid	child	KIDS TURN ON TEACHERS
link	connection	MAFIA LINK SCANDAL BREAKS
loom	approach, threaten	STRIKE LOOMS
man	representative	CLINTON MAN IN ISRAEL
mob	large gang, crowd	MOB ATTACKS KILLER
net	total	DRUG RAID NETS £1M
ordeal	painful experience, drama	JAIL ORDEAL ENDS
oust	push out, drive out, replace	BOSNIA OUSTS SERBS
output	production	INDUSTRIAL OUTPUT INCREASES
pact	agreement, treaty	PEACE PACT ENDS
pay	wages, salary	PAY RISE FOR MINERS
peril	danger	FLU PERIL
pit	coal mine	PIT TALKS END
plea	request for help	PLEA FOR BLOOD
pledge	promise	UNION PLEDGES SUPPORT
plunge	steep fall	DOLLAR PLUNGES
poll	election, opinion survey	POLL SHOWS SWING TO RIGHT
press for	demand, ask for	TEACHERS PRESS FOR PAY RISE
probe	investigation, investigate	VIAGRA TO BE PROBED
quit	resign, leave	DIRECTOR QUITS
quiz	interrogate	MINISTER QUIZZED
raid	attack, robbery	$23 M BANK RAID
rap	strong criticism	UNION RAP
riddle	mystery, puzzling incident	CORPSE RIDDLE
row	dispute, disagreement, argument	MINISTER QUITS IN ROW
scare	fear, public alarm, panic	BSE SCARE HITS EUROPE
seek	request	FLOOD VILLAGE SEEKS ACTION
slam	criticise severely	OPPOSITION SLAMMED
smash	break up, destroy	DRUGS RING SMASHED
snub	turn down, reject	BMW BID SNUBBED
soar	increase dramatically	WALL STREET SOARS
split	divide	EURO SPLITS COALITION
squeeze	shortage, scarcity	PETROL SQUEEZE IN BOSNIA
storm	violent dispute	TAXATION STORM GROWS
strife	conflict	PARTY STRIFE THREATENS PEACE
switch	change, deviation	SWITCH IN TRADE BALANCE
swoop	sudden attack or raid	DRUG SWOOP IN MAYFAIR
talks	discussions	PEACE TALKS THREATENED
toll	number of people killed	TOLL RISES TO 98 IN ESHEDE

top	exceed	TELECOM PROFITS TOP £40 M
tragedy	fatal accident	GUN TRAGEDY
urge	to recommend strongly	BLAIR URGES INQUIRY
vow	promise	WIDOW VOWS VENGEANCE
walkout	strike (often unofficial)	HOSPITAL WALKOUT
wed	marry	DIANA TO WED DODI
woo	try to win the favour of	SPD WOOS PDS

Appendix B

Advertisement abbreviations

Property advertisements

Abbr.	Meaning	Abbr.	Meaning
avail.	available	kit.	kitchen
balc.	balcony	lnge.	lounge
bed.	bedroom	lrge.	large
c.h.	central heating	min.	minute (small)
col.	coloured	mod.	modern
com.	communal	o.n.o.	or nearest offer
cond.	condition	p.b.	purpose-built
cpts.	carpets	pkg.	parking
ctns.	curtains	prop.	property
dble.	double	recr.	recreation
dec.	decorated	sep.	separate
fit.	fitted	shwr.	shower
flr.	floor	sngle.	single
gdn.	garden	stn.	station
gge.	garage	terr.	terraced
inc.	including		

Entertainment advertisements

adm.	admission	Einlaß
avail.	available	verfügbar
bkble.	bookable	zu reservieren
bkgs.	bookings	Reservierungen
cont.	continuous	fortlaufend
dly.	daily	täglich
evgs.	evenings	abends
exhib.	exhibition	Ausstellung
inc.	including	inklusive
mat.	matinee	Nachmittagsvorstellung
perf.	performance	Vorstellung
progr.	programme	Programm
sep.	separate	extra, getrennt
wk.	week	Woche
wkly.	weekly	wöchentlich

Appendix C

Word building

Wir haben Ihnen Wortbausteine zusammengestellt, die Ihnen in Fachtexten immer wieder begegnen werden. Sie helfen Ihnen beim Erschließen unbekannter Wörter. Man muß sie nicht auswendig können, es genügt, wenn man sie beim Lesen wiedererkennt. Weil sie so häufig sind, gehen sie dem "Vielleser" bald in Fleisch und Blut über und ver vielfachen seinen passiven Wortschatz.

1. Vorsilben und ihre Bedeutung

prefix	meaning	example	translation
ante	before	anteroom	Vorraum
anti	against	antipathy	Abneigung
bene	good; well	benefactor; benefit	Wohltäter; Gewinn
bi	two; twice	bilingual; bigamy	zweisprachig; Bigamie
circum	around; all around	circumference; circumstances	Umfang; Umstände
com; con; col	together; with	combine; collect	kombinieren; sammeln
contra; contro	against	controversial; controversy	umstritten; Streit
de	away from	depart; departure; devalue	abreisen; Abreise; abwerten
dia	across; through	dialogue; diameter	Dialog; Durchmesser
dis; di	apart; apart from	dislocate; displace	ausrenken; verpflanzen
dis	opposite; absence of	disinformation; discourage	Desinformation; entmutigen
hyper	over; above	hypersensitive	überempfindlich
inter	between; among	intervene; international	einschreiten; zwischenstaatlich
mal	bad; inadequate	malfunction	nicht richtig funktionieren
mis	wrong	misunderstand; mismanagement	mißverstehen
multi	many; much	multimedia; multitude	Menge
per	through	perforate	durchlöchern
pre	before	precede; preface	vorangehen; Vorwort
pro	before; forward	proceed; promote	vorgehen; befördern
re	again; back	repeat; repay	wiederholen; zurückzahlen
retro	backward	retrospective	Rückblick
sub; subter	below	subterranean	unterirdisch
syn; sym	with	sympathetic	mitfühlend
trans; tra	across	translate; transplant	übersetzen; verpflanzen
ultra	outside; extremely	ultrasonic; ultramodern	Überschall-; hoch--modern

un	not; reversal of action	unfinished; undo	unfertig; rückgängig machen
vice	one who takes the place of	vice-president; vice-chairman	stellvertretender Vorsitzender
with	against; back	withstand; withhold	widerstehen; zurückhalten

2. Die Wurzel der Wörter

root	meaning	example	translation
agr	farm	agriculture	Landwirtschaft
al	nourish	alimentary; alimony	nahrhaft; Unterhalts-zahlungen
alter	another; change	alternate current; alteration	Wechselstrom; Änderung
am	love	amiable; amateur	liebenswürdig; Liebhaber
ann	year	annual; annuity	jährlich; Jahresrente
aud	hear	audience; audition	Zuhörerschaft; Anhörung
aug	increase	augment; auction	vermehren; Auktion
brevi	short	abbreviate; brevity	abkürzen; Kürze
capit	head	capital; decapitate	Kapital; Hauptstadt, ent-haupten
celer	fast	accelerate	beschleunigen
cent	hundred	century	Jahrhundert
cess	go	accession; recession	Zugang; Rückgang
charg	load	cargo; discharge	Ladung; entladen
civ	citizen; city	civilisation; civilian	Zivilisation; Zivilist
clar	clear	clarify; declaration	verdeutlichen; Erklärung
crat	rule, government	democrat; autocratic	Demokrat; selbstherrlich
cri	judge	criteria; critic; crisis	Beurteilungsmaßstäbe; Kritiker
cumul	add to	accumulate	anhäufen
cur, curs	run	concur; current; excursion	zusammentreffen; laufend; Ausflug
da; don	give	donation; data	Schenkung; Daten
dec	ten	decade; decimal	Jahrzehnt
dem	people	democracy; demagogue	Volksherrschaft; Volksverführer
duc	lead	deduce; reduce to	abführen; absetzen (Steuer); zurückführen auf
eco	home	economy; ecology	Wirtschaft; Ökologie
fac	make; do	facility; manufacture	Anlage; herstellen
fer	carry	transfer; confer	übertragen; verleihen
fin	end	infinite; final	unendlich; schließlich
firm	strong	affirm; confirm	bekräftigen; bestätigen
flat	blow	deflate; inflate	entleeren; aufblähen

gram	written	telegram; diagram	Telegramm; Diagramm
hab	have	habit; exhibit; ability	Gewohnheit; ausstellen
her	stick	inherent; coherent; adhesive	innewohnend; zusammenhängend; haftend
integr	whole	integrate; integrity; integer	vereinigen; Unversehrtheit
journ	day	journal; journey; adjourn	Tageblatt; (Tages-)Reise; vertagen
leg	law	legislative; legal	gesetzgebend; rechtmäßig
manu	hand	manual; manufacture	Handbuch; herstellen
mere	trade	merchant; market	Händler; Markt
mis; mit	send	submit	unterbreiten; unterwerfen
nom	name	nominate; nominal value	berufen; Nennwert
nomy	system	economy	Wirtschaft(-system)
nov	new	novelty; renovate; innovate	Neuheit; erneuern; Neuerungen einführen
pan	all	company; companion	Gesellschaft
petit	seek	petition; competitor	Gesuch; Mitbewerber
preci	price	precious; appreciate	kostbar; wertschätzen
rog	ask	interrogate; arrogant	befragen; anmaßend
rupt	break	bankrupt	ruiniert
script	write	description; ascribe	Beschreibung; zuschreiben
sist	stand	resist; consist of; persist	widerstehen; bestehen aus; fortbestehen
sper	hope	desperate; despair; prosper	verzweifelt; verzweifeln; gedeihen
spect	watch; look	spectator; inspect	Betrachter; besichtigen
temp	time	temporal; contemporary	zeitweilig; Zeitgenosse
test	witness	testify	bezeugen
vac	empty	vacant; vacancy	leer, unbesetzt; freie Stelle
vari	different	variety; various	Vielfalt; verschieden(e)
vid; vis	sight	revise; revision	überarbeiten; Durchsicht; Korrektur

3. Nachsilben und ihre Bedeutung

suffix	**meaning**	**example**	**translation**
able; ible; ble	able to	curable; flexible; portable	heilbar; biegsam; tragbar
acity	having the quality of	capacity; vivacity	Fassungsvermögen; Lebhaftigkeit
ance	process or action	performance; appearance	Vorführung; Auftreten

ancy; ency	state or condition	vacancy; dependency	Leerstelle; Abhängigkeit
an; ant	belong to; act as	statistician; accountant	Statistiker; Buchhalter
ion, tion, ation	action; state of	union; information; combination	Vereinigung; Auskunft; Zusammenführung
ee	one acted upon	employee; trainee	Angestellter; Auszubildender
fy	to make or render	mystify; simplify	hinters Licht führen; vereinfachen
hood	condition	boyhood; priesthood	Kindheit; Priesterschaft
ine	procedure; art	medicine; discipline	Heilkunde; Sparte
ious	full of	precious; delicious	wertvoll; köstlich
ish	like	foolish; childish	töricht; kindisch
less	without	flawless; homeless	fehlerfrei; heimatlos
ment	result; action	development; fragment	Entwicklung
ness	little	forgetfulness; sadness	Vergeßlichkeit; Traurigkeit
ory	place of	factory; dormitory	Produktionsstätte; Schlafsaal
uos; uous	full of	dangerous; mysterious	gefahrvoll; geheimnisvoll
ure	process	procedure; departure	Verfahren; Abreise
ward	direction	backward; heavenward	rückwärts; himmelwärts
y	characterised by	sleepy; stinky	schläfrig; übelriechend

Adapted from *Webster's New Encyclopedic Dictionary*, Könemann, Köln

Key to the Exercises

CHAPTER 1

The battle for the beaches

Task 1: Scanning for keywords

an all inclusive holiday	*package tour*
travel agency	*tour operator*
very low prices	*cut-throat prices*

Task 2: In other words

These Germans reserve chairs *in great numbers.*	These Germans reserve chairs *in bulk.*
That'll *spark off* some comments when they come back.	That'll *trigger off* some comments when they come back.
If you want to *fight* about chairs, do it by yourself.	If you want to *battle* about chairs, do it by yourself.
We have the *best* tour operators in the world.	We have the most *efficient* tour operators in the world.
You're efficient at *reserving* chairs anyway.	You're efficient at *snapping up* chairs anyway.

Task 3: Complete the business idioms

Ladies and Gentlemen,
We'd hoped our advertising campaign would *trigger off* an enormous public response and that smokers would *snap up* our fat-burning, green cigar. As you know this has not been the case and we were forced to *bring down* the price. Let's take this product off the market to *cut* our losses.

Task 4: Wordfinder's corner

verb	**noun**	**noun**	**adjective**
penetrate	penetration	*efficiency*	efficient
operate	operator	*cheapness*	cheap
compete	competition	*identity*	identical

Task 5: Guesswork

1 A, 2 C, 3 A, 4 A, 5 C, 6 C A

Task 6: Scanning for figures

What percentage of the seats do UK charters fill on each tour?	95 %
What percentage of the seats do German charters fill on each tour?	75 %
By what percentage are UK operators cheaper than German companies?	30 %

Task 7: Guided note-taking practice

The British travel industry is a danger for German operators because

1. British travel companies are the	*largest*
2. British charter airlines are the	*most efficient*
3. Competition in Britain is	*cut-throat*
4. Competition in Germany is	*limited*
5. British charters	*fill 95 percent of the seats*
6. They buy hotel rooms	*in bulk*
7. They offer package tours	*thirty percent cheaper*
8. The price advantage is	*crucial*

Task 8: Skimming exercise

1 B, 2 E, 3 C, 4 A, 5 D

CHAPTER 2

Euromania

Task 1: Scanning for keywords

criteria standards specifications

Task 2: In other words

Guinness doesn't *fulfil* the specifications.	Guinness doesn't *meet* the specifications.
Under to the German law it's not a beer.	*According to* German law it's not a beer.
I've to *remind* you *of* the rules.	I've to *refer* you *to* the rules.
Euro-MPs wanted to *classify* cheese.	Euro-MPs wanted to *grade* cheese.
The European Commission *decided* to call it vegelate.	The European Commission *decreed* to call it vegelate.
I have to refer you to the *regulations.*	I have to refer you to the *rules*.

Task 3: Complete the business idioms

meet	the terms of a contract	Vertragsbedingungen erfüllen
	the delivery deadline	Lieferfrist einhalten
	the customer needs	Kundenbedürfnisse befriedigen
	the EC-norm	EC-Norm erfüllen
	precise specifications	genaue Normen einhalten

Task 4: Wordfinder's corner

noun	verb	adjective	noun
specification	*specify*	long	*length*
standard	*standardise*	wide	*width*
classification	*classify*	high	*height*
qualification	*qualify*	bushy	*bushiness*

Task 5: Guesswork

1 B, 2 A, 3 A, 4 B, 5 C, 6 A

Task 6: Getting the gist

The article is about the
attempt to have strict
norms on Christmas trees
adopted by the CEN

Task 7: Scanning for the author's standpoint

The author is against the attempt to have a strict norms on Christmas trees adopted by the CEN. He uses irony when he says: *"All clear? Perhaps it will be more so to the officials of the European Normalisation Committee."*

CHAPTER 3

When jokes backfire

Task 1: Scanning for keywords

make someone feel uncomfortable	*embarrass*
correct or suitable for a situation	*appropriate*
be an inseparable part or quality	*inherent*
an instrument to fight with	*weapon*
a group of listeners	*audience*

Task 2: In other words

A joke that *is not funny.*	A joke that *falls flat.*
A good joke *makes me laugh.*	A good joke *cracks me up.*
Sex is *part of* all your jokes.	Sex is *inherent* in all your jokes.
Such jokes can *hurt feelings.*	Such jokes can *cause offence.*
Jokes can be a *two-edged sword.*	Jokes can be a *weapon* that backfires.
Stop *pulling my leg*!	Stop *teasing* me!

Task 3: Complete the idioms: One verb – five phrases

verb	plus phrase	meaning
save	face	not to be embarrassed
	the day	solve the problem
	the situation	find a solution
	someone trouble	do someone a service
	up for retirement	put aside money for later

Task 4: Wordfinder's corner

verb	noun	verb	noun
assume	*assumption*	die	*death*
believe	*belief*	embarrass	*embarrassment*

Task 5: Do you know the German 'Fremdwort'?

English	German	English	German
inherent	*inhärent*	equivalent	*Äquivalent*
misplaced	*deplaziert*	routinely	*routinemäßig*
determine	*determinieren*	adequately	*adäquat*

Task 6: Guesswork

1A, 2B, 3AC, 4BA, 5CB,6C

Task 7: Did you get the message?

1F, 2F, 3T, 4T

Task 8: Getting the gist

Thesis: Humour is a *powerful weapon.* However, managers often do *not know how to use it* on the international stage.

Warning: Jokes that are *appropriate in one* country can *cause offence / confusion* in *another* country.

Examples: Germany. jokes are *used to improve the working climate* rather than in serious discussions.
France: jokes should not be used *with higher-ranking persons.*
Asia: jokes can easily make your partners *lose face.*

CHAPTER 4

Supermarkets the American way

Task 1: Scanning for keywords

A. Food

the most important food of a nation:	*staple food*
kind of food a person eats every day:	*diet*
type of food, also a plate:	*dish*

B. Around the supermarket

individual store of a chain:	*outlet*
where you pay for your food:	*checkout*
company that sells goods to the public:	*retailer*
product made by a particular company:	*brand*
reduction in price:	*discount*

Task 2: In other words

Handelsyard has been *bought* by Wal-Mart.	Handelsyard has been *taken over* by Wal-Mart.
Well, *let's wait and see* ...	Well, it *remains to be seen* ....
They *provide food for* a very conservative taste.	They *cater to* a very conservative taste.
How does the *variety of food* here compare with back in England?	How does the *choice* here compare with back in England?
They only go for a limited number of *products*.	They only go for a limited number of *brands*.

Task 3: Complete the business idioms: One verb – five phrases

bring	about better service	besseren Service einführen
	down prices	Preise herunterbringen
	in an expert	Experten heranziehen
	into service	in Dienst stellen
	to an end	zu Ende bringen

Task 4: Wordfinder's corner

verb	noun	verb	noun
employ	*employee*	associate	*association*
choose	*choice*	shop	*shopper*

Task 5: Guesswork

1B, 2B, 3C, 4 A, 5 B, 6 A

Task 6: Did you get the message?

1 F, 2 T, 3 F, 4 T

Task 7: Scanning for the author's standpoint

1 B, 2 B, 3 complacent (selbstgefällig, zufrieden) **4 A, 5** addiction to high profit margins (Sucht nach hohen Gewinnspannen)

CHAPTER 5

Prince joins battle for language

Task 1: Scanning for keywords

when we have rivals in business we are in	*competition*
say or do things that cause fear	*threaten*
slice or part of the market	*share*
expand (into a new area)	*spread*
stress or emphasise	*highlight*

Task 2: In other words

They've got a good *knowledge* of the *language.*	They've got a good *command* of the *vernacular.*
I think we *are not as popular as we think.*	I think we *overestimate* our popularity.
American business is *expanding* everywhere.	American business is *spreading* everywhere.
That could be an *amazing* number of people.	That could be a *staggering* number of people.

Task 3: Complete the business idioms: One verb – five idioms

spread	a rumour	Gerücht verbreiten
	one's business everywhere	Geschäfte ausweiten
	payments over two years	Zahlungen strecken
	a strike to other companies	Streik ausweiten
	the costs over a year	Kosten verteilen

Task 4: Wordfinder's corner

give one's *backing* to	give one's *support* to
the American *vernacular*	the American *English*
a *lucrative* market	a *profitable* market
a *growth* industry	an *expanding* industry
maintain a position	*keep* a position
the figures are *staggering*	the figures are *amazing*
maintain the quality	*preserve* the quality

Find the noun

threaten	*threat*
compete	*competition*
produce	*product*

Task 5: Guesswork

1 A, 2 C, 3 B, 4 A, 5 C, 6 A, 7 A, 8 C

Task 6: The article in a nutshell

The Prince of Wales *launched* a campaign to *preserve* 'proper English' as a world *leader*. He *highlighted/emphasised* the threat to Britain's position in the lucrative language-teaching *market* from the *spread* of American English. He emphasised the *need* to *maintain* the quality of language. The countries of the Pacific Rim will be among the main *targets* of a campaign to *develop* new *products* and use the Internet to widen *access* to English courses.

CHAPTER 6

How to kick-start Germany's economy

Task 1: Scanning for keywords

The *important* thing is to become flexible.	*crucial*
They argue that it makes the company more *efficient.*	*competitive*
We need to improve *efficiency* at universities.	*standards*
Shall their tax *load* be reduced?	*burden*
And that's good for the *expansion* of industry.	*growth*

Task 2: In other words

There are other reasons like the famous *stock exchange rate.*	There are other reasons like the famous *shareholder value.*
What other solutions did he *propose* for Germany's problems?	What other solutions did he *suggest* for Germany's problems?
But the *task* is to find a government that will carry out these tax reforms.	But the *challenge* is to find a government that will carry out these tax reforms.

Task 3: Complete the business idioms: One verb – five idioms

carry	out tax reforms	Steuerreformen durchführen
	forward a debt	Schulden vortragen
	on business through ads	Geschäft betreiben
	aims through to the end	Ziele verwirklichen
	away with enthusiasm	in Begeisterung steigern

Task 4: Wordfinder's corner

Find a word that means the opposite

secure jobs	insecure jobs
increase costs	reduce costs
avoid reforms	implement reforms

Find a word that has a similar meaning

propose reforms	*suggest* reforms
keep a position	*maintain* a position
raise standards	*improve* standards
lower tax burdens	*cut* tax burdens
create growth	*generate* growth

Find four words that have the same root

compete { competitor, competition, competitive, competitiveness

Task 5: Guesswork

1 C A, 2 B, 3 A, 4 C

Task 6: Choose a word that fills the gap

1 B, 2 C, 3 A

Task 7: Complete the key phrases

1. Lasting reforms must be *implemented.*
2. New opportunities need to be *explored.*
3. Research and technology must be *exploited.*
4. Service and customer relations have to be *improved.*
5. The tax burden on German businesses has to be *lowered.*
6. Qualifications at schools and universities must be *improved.*

CHAPTER 7

Destress in salt water

Task 1: Scanning for keywords

veins and arteries of the heart	*cardiovascular system*
manager in a key position	*executive*
middle of your body	*abdomen*
in harmony	*in tune*

Task 2: In other words

Are you under a lot of *stress*?	Are you under a lot of *pressure*?
If you're stressed or anxious you build fat around your *middle.*	If you're stressed or anxious you build fat around your *abdomen.*
Some people do *grow old* when put *under* pressure.	Some people do *shrivel* when *exposed* to pressure.
Get rid of your poisons.	*You've got to detox.*
There's another method for people *with a tendency* to putting on fat.	There's another method for people *susceptible* to putting on fat.
Fill your bath full of salt water and *lie* naked in it.	Fill your bath full of salt water and *float* naked in it.

Task 3: Complete the business idioms: One verb – five idioms

put	in sixty hours a week	sechzig Stunden investieren
	the record straight	für klare Verhältnisse sorgen
	him in the picture	ins Bild setzen
	pressure on	Druck machen
	on weight	Gewicht darauf legen

Task 4: Wordfinder's corner

Find a word that means the opposite

stress	*destress*	cognitive	*physical*
shrivel	*thrive*	increase	*reduce*

Find a word that has a similar meaning

mind	*soul*	belly	*abdomen*
relax	*destress*	rise	*increase*
illness	*disease*	stress	*strain*
answer	*response*	out of tune	out of *sync*

Find the noun

execute	*executive/execution*
respond	*response*
float	*flotation*
relax	*relaxation*
harmonise	*harmony*

Task 5: Guesswork

1 B, 2 A, 3 B, C, 4 C, 5 A

Task 6: Did you get the meaning?

Are these statements true or false?

1. Some people need stress to be successful.	T
2. Anxious people tend to put on weight.	T
3. Cardiovascular disease is a disease of the soul.	F
4. Stress hormones protect the body's defence system.	T
5. Floating in salt water is the equivalent of a good night's rest.	F

CHAPTER 8

The Elk test

Task 1: Scanning for keywords

very usual or normal	*commonplace*
dirty or blacken something	*smear*
solution for putting things right	*remedy*
comparison of systems of the same type	*bench-marking*

Task 2: In other words

The fastest vehicle on *its side.*	The fastest vehicle on *one door.*
There's a *great demand for* ESP.	There's a *boom* in ESP.
FV and Polec have also *marketed* new models.	FV and Polec have also *launched* new models.
They call it *bench-marking test against rival cars.*	They call it *competition* testing.
All cars would *topple* over when put through this sort of test.	All cars would *tip* or *flip* over when put through this sort of test.

Task 3: Complete the business idioms: One verb – five idioms

put	through a test	einem Test unterziehen
	off until later	auf später verschieben
	into perspective	zurechtrücken
	up the money for a project	das Geld aufbringen
	down on paper	zu Papier bringen

Task 4: Wordfinder's corner

Find a word that has a similar meaning.

market (v)	*launch*	competing model	*rival model*
solution	*remedy*	prestige	*reputation*
maker	*manufacturer*	rise rapidly	*boom*
tip	*topple*	control, measure	*gauge*

Task 5: Words in context

1. A high-speed swerve is certainly something that every *manufacturer* believes it must put its cars through.
2. They wanted to smear the good *reputation* of Opel.
3. High-tech *remedies* are emerging.
4. As Daimler saw its reputation threatened, it conducted a 'bench-marking test' against *rival* models.

Task 6: Guesswork

1 C A,2 C, 3 B

Task 7: Did you get the meaning?

Are these statements true or false?

1.	Elk tests are not absolutely necessary.	**T**
2.	Opel denied testing the Golf.	**F**
3.	The Golf went through the test without toppling over.	**F**
4.	Computerised balancing systems are selling well.	**T**
5.	All elk-tested German cars tipped and flipped.	**T**
6.	Opel was the first to tip over a Golf.	**F**

Task 8: Scanning for the author's standpoint

1 B, 2 C, 3 A

CHAPTER 9

The price of beauty

Task 1: Scanning for keywords

being very fat indeed	*obese*
eat up all of something	*consume*
a stamp which gives the okay	*approval*
you buy it at the stock exchange	*share*

Task 2: In other words

I won't say you're *fat,* Robert.	I won't say you're *obese,* Robert.
There's too *big a quantity* of fat on you.	There's too *much excess* fat on you.
This will be a *shock* for you.	This will be a *body blow* for you.
The *final result* is that my chest has dropped one metre down to my stomach.	The *bottom line* is that my chest has dropped one metre down to my stomach.

The bits and pieces have *moved to another place*.	The bits and pieces have *shifted*.
Roche are bringing out a new wonder drug, a *fatbuster*.	Roche are bringing out a new wonder drug, a *fatburner*.

Task 3: Complete the business idioms: One verb – five idioms

take	the world by storm	die Welt im Sturm erobern
	a body blow	einen Tiefschlag einstecken
	over a company	eine Firma übernehmen
	firm action on	energisch vorgehen
	risks	Risiken eingehen

Task 4: Wordfinder's corner

Find a word that has a similar meaning.

transpiration	*sweat*	prophecy	*forecast*
fatburner	*fatbuster*	put on the market	*launch*
eat	*consume*	estimated to be fat	*deemed to be fat*
barrier	*hurdle*	last but one	*penultimate*

Find the noun

approve	*approval*	Zustimmung
exceed	*excess*	Überschuß
compete	*competitor*	Konkurrent
obese	*obesity*	Fettleibigkeit
advise	*adviser/advice*	Ratgeber
prescribe	*prescription*	Rezept (Arzt)

Task 5: Words in context

1. The American drugs agency did not give its *approval* to the product.
2. What level of profit do you *forecast* for next year?
3. All your *excess* fat must be reduced by dieting.
4. You can buy Xenical on *prescription*.
5. All your *competitors* have patents for similar drugs, too.

Task 6: Guesswork

1 C, 2 B, 3 C, 4 A

Task 7: Scanning for facts and figures

1. Xenical might enjoy peak sales of SF *700* million a year.
2. More than *100* million people worldwide are obese.
3. Obesity: a body mass index of more than *30* kg/m^2.

4. More than *30* per cent of Americans are obese.
5. Up to *20* per cent of the adult population in Europe are estimated to be fat.
6. The market for Xenical could be worth $*50* billion.

Task 8: Scanning for the author's standpoint

1 C, 2 take a body-blow, feel the pinch, betting, 3 A, 4 B

CHAPTER 10

BSE or the mad cow disease

Task 1: Scanning for keywords

information, a mixture of truth and untruth	*rumour*
say arrogant things about oneself	*boast*
stand, suffer or tolerate	*endure*
a feeling of mistrust	*suspicion*
stories circulate	*get around*

Task 2: In other words

That's only *making yourself important.*	That's just *boasting.*
Don't *say it's not true,* Mick.	Don't *deny it,* Mick.
Raising all those animals for greedy humans!	*Breeding* all those animals for greedy humans!
There've been several cases *getting* around.	There've been several cases *circulating* around.
You can't *tolerate* anything about Germany.	You can't *endure* anything about Germany.

Task 3: Complete the business idioms: One verb – five idioms

get	a message around	eine Nachricht verbreiten
	worked up	sich aufregen
	a message across	klar machen
	down to business	Arbeit anfangen
	under control	kontrollieren

Task 4: Wordfinder's corner

Find a word that has the opposite meaning

experts *accepted* claims	experts *denied* claims
lose one's reputation	*retain* one's reputation
weaken suspicions	*strengthen* suspicions

Find a word that has a similar meaning

home-bred cattle	*domestically-bred* cattle
give full explanation	*provide* full explanation
keep one's reputation	*retain* one's reputation
a *controversial* BSE case	a *disputed* BSE case
clearly under-reported	*grossly* under-reported
efforts to *lift* a ban	*attempts* to *ease* a ban

Task 5: A little newspaper grammar

a beast that has been called Anita	a beast *called Anita*
a cow that was infected with BSE	a cow *infected* with BSE
has been found in Bavaria	found in Bavaria
an animal which was imported	an animal *imported*
from Switzerland	from Switzerland

Task 6: Guesswork

1 A, 2 C, 3 B, 4 AC, 5 C, 6 A

Task 7: Did you get the meaning?

Are these statements facts (F) or claims (C)?

1. Six BSE cows have been found in Germany.	F
2. No link between Anita and any Swiss cow has been found.	C
3. BSE cows have been under-reported in Europe.	C
4. Anita was an import from Switzerland.	C
5. There are no home-bred BSE cows in Germany.	C

CHAPTER 11

Buba and the Euro

Task 1: Scanning for keywords

money of a country	*currency*
a coming together of things	*convergence*
something hard and inflexible	*rigid*
an idea or action which totally fails	*flop*
group of countries with a central government	*union*

Task 2: In other words

It'll be better when we have the *single currency.*	It'll be better when we have the *monetary union.*
The *signs are* that only four or five countries qualify.	The *implications* are that only four or five countries qualify.
Germany has *continual* problems with its unemployment.	Germany has *persistent* problems with its unemployment.

Task 3: Complete the business idioms: One verb – five idioms

give	up one's currency	seine Währung aufgeben
	careful consideration (to)	sorgfältig überlegen
	someone the sack	jemanden feuern, entlassen
	and take	geben und nehmen
	out false information	Fehlinformationen liefern

Task 4: Wordfinder's corner

Find a word that has the opposite meaning.

overstatement	*understatement*
quiet	*disquiet*
temporary	*persistent*
flexibility	*rigidity*
success	*flop*

Find a word that has a similar meaning.

important	*significant*
single currency	*monetary union*
deliver a judgement	*deliver a verdict*
adequate warnings	*appropriate warnings*
finally	*ultimately*
have consequences	*have implications*

Task 5: Guided translation

1. *Entry* into monetary union will have *significant economic implications.*
2. The Buba *delivered its verdict* on the birth of the Euro.
3. The document is a *masterpiece of understatement*.
4. If the Euro is a *terrible flop* then the Buba can *pull out* its document and say: "We told you so."
5. Measures with a *temporary effect* have been used by Italy and France to enable them to meet Maastricht reference values.
6. *Persistent* unemployment reflects rigidities which are a *long-term burden* for the future *stability policy.*

Task 6: Scanning for hard words

A. unemployment *goes on and on*?	*persistent*
B. a country's position can *be kept at the same level*?	*sustainable*
C. choosing participants is *finally* a political decision?	*ultimately*
D. it is the Buba's *lifework*?	*opus*

Task 7: Did you get the meaning?

Are these statements true (T) or false (F)?

1. The Buba made a clear decision about the Euro.	**F**
2. The Buba took some risks with its verdict.	**F**
3. The Buba had some problems to arrive at its comment.	**T**
4. Britain has low unemployment because it is flexible.	**T**

Task 8: Sensing style

Are they allusions to the Bible?

1. There was much gnashing of teeth.	**Yes**
2. The bank can claim credit ...	**No**
3. And the Buba spoke ...	**Yes**
4. And the Buba looked, and saw it was no good.	**Yes**

CHAPTER 12

Nike versus Adidas

Task 1: Scanning for keywords

listeners	*audience*
equipment	*kit*
programme on the air	*broadcast*
someone who watches TV	*viewer*
support a product with money	*sponsor*
someone who profits by an action	*beneficiary*

Task 2: In other words

You have to *look after* your own real needs.	You have to *square up* to your own real needs.
You've been *tricked* by advertising.	You've been *ambushed* by advertising.
I know there's a *lot of demand* in this market.	I know there's a *boom* in this market.

Task 3: Complete the business idioms: sign and step

1. The old chairman *stepped down* because of the company's losses.
2. The bank *stepped in* to save the company from bankruptcy.
3. John, one of the directors, *stepped into* the old chairman's shoes.
4. He managed to *step up* production again.
5. John *signed up* three new production managers.
6. He *signed over* some of the buildings for use as offices.
7. He had to *sign away* his right to the money.

Task 4: Wordfinder's corner

the *competition* is bitter	*rivalry* is bitter
supporter of a club	*sponsor* of a club
set up a football village	*erect* a football village
six international *teams*	six international *squads*
get ready to fight	*square up* to fight
react by doing something	*respond* by doing something

Task 5: Words in context

1. They are *squaring up* to fight for the largest *audience* on the planet.
2. It has also sponsored the *kit* of nine teams.
3. Adidas will *erect* a football village under the Eiffel Tower.
4. Nike has *sponsored* six international *squads*.
5. Adidas has *signed up* Paul Gascoigne, Paul Ince and David Beckham.
6. Nike has *responded* by planning a site outside the city.

Task 6: Guesswork

1 BA, 2 C, 3 AA, 4 B, 5 C, 6 AC, 7 A

Task 7: Scanning for figures

To how many countries will the 1998 World Cup be broadcast ?	195
How many million viewers will watch each game worldwide?	500
How many official sponsors will be admitted to the 1998 World Cup?	12
How many international teams has Nike sponsored?	6
How many international teams has Adidas sponsored?	9

Task 8: Did you get the meaning?

Are these statements true (T) or false (F)?

1. Nike and Adidas target their campaigns at the spectators who come to the World Cup finals. **F**
2. Nike and Adidas are among the twelve official sponsors of the World Cup. **F**
3. The Olympic Committee will prevent Nike from buying up all poster sites in Paris. **F**
4. Nike is going to erect a football village in Paris. **F**

CHAPTER 13

Transparent man

Task 1: Scanning for keywords

be against something	*oppose*
illegally copy passports	*forge* passports
most modern technology	*state-of-the-art* technology
make known secret plans	*reveal* secret plans

Task 2: In other words

You Texans are *living in the past.*	You Texans are *old-fashioned.*
The system doesn't *accept* your palm print.	The system doesn't *recognise* your palm print.
There's nobody quite like you.	You're *unique.*

Task 3: Our business idioms: cut, do, carry

Can you match idiom with meaning?

1	cut the need to do it	E	etwas überflüssig machen
2	cut queues by a half	B	Warteschlangen halbieren
3	do away with passports	A	Pässe abschaffen
4	carry credit cards	C	Kreditkarten besitzen
5	cut wages	D	Löhne senken
6	do business with	F	Geschäfte machen mit

And now put the right idiom in the right context.

1. They are thinking of *cutting wages* to be more competitive.
2. You've failed to *carry out* your agreement to repay the bank loan.
3. The government can't *do away with* civil liberties.
4. He is not a frank and open character. If I were you I wouldn't *do business with* him.

Task 4: Wordfinder's corner

Find a word that has almost the same meaning as the words in *italics*.

pay with *plastic money*	pay by *credit card*
recognise a handprint	*identify* a handprint
do away with civil liberties	*remove* civil liberties
get access to an establishment	*gain* access to an establishment
put one's hand against a screen	*place* one's hand against a screen
shorten queues	*cut* queues

Find the opposite of the words in *italics*-

do away with civil liberties	*introduce* civil liberties
shorten queues	*lengthen* queues
keep plans *secret*	*reveal* plans
be in favour of the system	*oppose* the system
numbers will *fall* by 6 %	numbers will *rise/increase* by 6 %

Task 5: Business words in context

B: I was at the Car Show last week and saw your new Rolls Royce *revealed* for the first time. I was very impressed with it. Your company has *risen* in my estimation. There are, however, a few things I'm not clear about.

S: Well, thank you for your support. I hope we can *remove* any doubt you still have about the Rolls.

B: There's one thing. Could you *cut* the price a bit?

S: Everything is possible, but it'll have to be a cash payment, no *credit cards.*

B: And what about the maintenance? Do you think I'll be able to afford a Rolls?

S: Well, I'm afraid anybody who asks a question like that can't.

Task 6: Guesswork

1 A, 2 C, 3 C, 4 BA, 5 A

Task 7: Scanning for figures

Expected rise in passenger numbers per year:	6 per cent
How long will it take to get through immigration using handprint passports?	15 seconds
In how many years will a paper-based system be out of date?	in 50 years

Task 8: Guided note-taking practice

1. The new system is based on	*handprint recognition*
2. The handprint is converted	*into computerised code*
3. The information is placed	*on a magnetic strip*
4. A card contains	*matching details and data*

Task 9: Scanning for attitudes

1 A spy thriller, **B** state-of-the-art method **2** critical, **3** hopelessly old-fashioned, **5** introducing national identity cards by the back door

CHAPTER 14

Motorcar misery

Task 1: Scanning for keywords

get worse and worse	*deteriorate*
failure of a system	*breakdown*
a flat tyre of a car or bike	*puncture*

Task 2: In other words

The car's always been so *dependable.*	The car's always been so *reliable.*
The car *won't move another inch.*	The car's *broken down.*
That would really be a *prize for the losers.*	That would really be the *booby prize.*
VW has been *eliminated from* the list of reliable cars.	VW has been *struck off* the list of reliable cars.

Task 3: One verb – five business idioms

1. Most cars *strike trouble* during the first year.
2. VW has been *struck off* the list of the most reliable cars.
3. Automobile workers are *striking for* higher wages.
4. I struck *a good bargain.* I bought a second-hand Mitsubishi for $200.
5. Let's strike *a balance* and come to a fair decision.

Task 4: Wordfinder's corner

Find a word that has almost the same meaning as the words in *italics*.

have a breakdown	*suffer* a breakdown
quality has *deteriorated*	quality has *worsened*
make cars more *reliable*	make cars more *dependable*
get into trouble	*strike* trouble
put a model *on the market*	*launch* a model
the most improved *brand*	the most improved *make*

Find the opposite of the words in *italics*.

increase in performance	*decline* in performance
cars are becoming *reliable*	cars are becoming *troublesome*
a *worsening* compared with last year	an *improvement* compared with last year
double (v) the breakdowns per year	*halve* the breakdowns per year

Task 5: Words in context

1. Company cars are becoming more troublesome, with one in four models *suffering* a breakdown.
2. The *decline* in performance comes despite claims from producers.
3. Saab almost *halved* its breakdown count.
4. The best company car on the road is now a Jaguar, with just seven breakdowns per 100 vehicles – an *improvement* from 9.2 last year.
5. Second-place BMW *deteriorated* from 7.1 last year to 8.2 in 1997.
6. Mercedes *worsened* noticeably to 13.4 - which makes it less dependable than Fiat, Nissan and Honda.

Task 6: Car parts that may cause a breakdown

1	accelerator	H	Gaspedal
2	brake	C	Bremse
3	clutch	B	Kupplung
4	alternator	I	Verteiler
5	fan	D	Lüfter
6	carburettor	A	Vergaser
7	piston	F	Kolben
8	gear box	J	Getriebe
9	tyre	G	Reifen
10	radiator	E	Kühler

Task 7: Guesswork

1 A, 2 B, 3 C, 4 B, 5 A

Task 8: Working with the graph

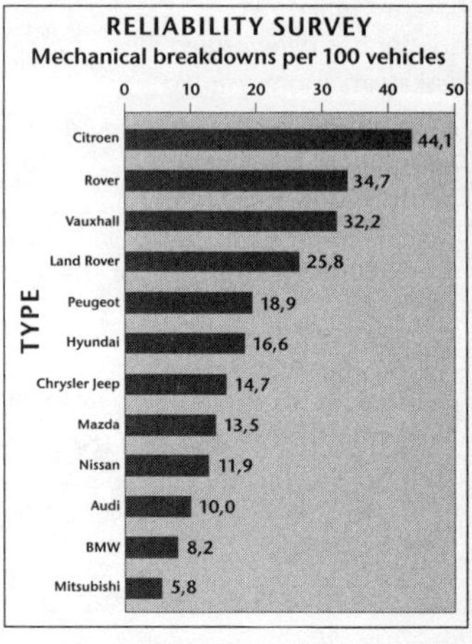

CHAPTER 15

The best meals in the skies

Task 1: Scanning for keywords

provide meals for guests commercially:	*cater*
cost of flight tickets:	*fare*
extra quality of services:	*value-added services*
a short period of time:	*spell*

Task 2: In other words

AAA has *found a gap in the market.*	AAA has *carved* itself a *niche.*
Flying passengers only *make up* 40 % of profit.	Flying passengers only *account for* 40 % of profit.
It's time for Swissair to *give up flying.*	It's time for Swissair to *hang up its flying suits.*

Task 3: Complete the business idioms

hang	up one's flying suits	Pilotenuniform an den Nagel hängen
	on to one's shares	Aktien halten
	in the balance	auf der Kippe stehen
	trophies all over the wall	Wände mit Trophäen behängen

Task 4: Wordfinder's corner

verb	**noun**	**German**
fly	flight	Flug
relieve	relief	Erleichterung
extend	extension	Ausweitung
think	thinker	Denker
analyse	analyst	Analytiker

Find words that have almost the same meaning.

find a market gap	*carve out a niche*
expand one's activities	*extend* (one's activities)
a *calm* thinker	a *quiet* thinker
warmed up meals	*reheated* meals
better *profits*	better *returns*
focus on services	*concentrate* on services
be used to warmed up meals	*be accustomed* to warmed up meals

Task 5: Guesswork

1 A, 2 B, 3 B, 4 C

Task 6: Did you get the meaning?

Are these statements true (T) or false (F)?

1. Swissair are giving up flying because it is too messy.	**F**
2. Catering is more profitable than flying passengers and cargo.	**T**
3. In 1997 flying passengers accounted for 50% of the profit.	**F**
4. Swissair will cook for other carriers.	**T**
5. Bruggisser used to be a financial controller at Union Bank of Switzerland.	**F**
6. Airline fares continue to fall.	**T**

Task 7: Guided note-taking practice

1. There is little *profit in flying passengers and cargo.*
2. There is more profit in *airline-related activities/catering.*
3. That is why Swissair *is going to give up flying.*

CHAPTER 16

Bullying bosses and the Nanny State

Task 1: Scanning for keywords

an official committee	*quango*
instructions or directives	*guidelines*
something that can be done is ...	*feasible*
push someone around because you're bigger	*bully*

Task 2: In other words

You're *not willing to work.*	You're *workshy.*
A worker can take *legal action against* his company.	A worker can *take* his company *to court.*
Actually, they should *take you to court.*	Actually, they should *prosecute* you.
You should pay *money as a penalty.*	You should pay a *fine.*
Rules should be *made stricter.*	*Guidelines* should be *put on a tighter footing.*

Task 3: Complete the business idioms

1. My boss doesn't want to *give* me *time off* for my wedding.
2. Workers should be allowed to *take time off* when their children are sick.
3. But they shouldn't *get time off* for shopping.
4. Bosses can be *taken to court* for *putting* their employees *under stress.*
5. The HSE wants to *put* rules *on a tighter footing.*

Task 4: Wordfinder's corner

Find the nouns.

prosecute	*prosecution*	injure	*injury*
feasible	*feasibility*	employ	*employer*

Find a word that has almost the same meaning as the words in *italics*.

bosses must face heavy *penalties*	bosses must face heavy *fines*
a Government-*financed committee*	a Government-*funded quango*
unsafe working conditions	*poor safeguards*
instructions are *given* to employers	*guidelines* are *issued* to employers
recognise varying degrees of stress	*identify* varying degrees of stress
calm down unions	*appease* unions
give someone a rocket	*deliver* a rocket to someone

Find the opposite of the words in *italics*.

legal	illegal
limited	unlimited
possible	impossible
loose	tight
healthy	sick/unhealthy

Task 5: Words in context

1. A Code of Practice which puts it on a *tighter* regulatory footing.
2. Bosses who *deliver* a rocket to workshy staff could end up in court.
3. *Guidelines* on stress are already *issued* to employers and employees.
4. It was *impossible* to say what the maximum *penalty* would be.
5. Workers have a legal right to time off if their children are *sick.*
6. Miss Harman's plan will be seen as an attempt to *appease* unions.

Task 6: Guesswork

1 C, 2 B, 3 A, 4 C, 5 C

Task 7: Did you get the message?

Are these statements true (T) or false (F)?

1. 500,000 employees claim to suffer stress. **T**
2. Guidelines on stress are already in place. **T**
3. Employers can be taken to court if they put workers under unfair stress. **F**
4. Employers have been fined for bullying. **F**

Task 8: Guided note-taking practice

According to the article the HSE ensures three workplace rights:

1. the right to *take time off to look after one's sick children*
2. the right to *work free from stress*
3. the right to *safety at the workplace*

CHAPTER 17

Shop around the clock

Task 1: Scanning for keywords

making statements about the future	*forecast / predict*
gradually remove or rub away	*erode*
compensate	*offset*
boring, everyday work	*chores*

Task 2: In other words

That's our *style* of life.	That's our *pattern* of life.
Irregular working hours will *wear* family life *away.*	Irregular working hours will *erode* family life.
You *spread* the *jobs* over several people.	You *distribute* the *chores* over several people.
We *had no time for anything.*	We were *rushed off our feet.*

Task 3: Our business idiom: lead

Can you match idiom with meaning?

1	lead to	**D**	have as a result
2	lead the field	**A**	be best / first
3	lead on	**B**	deceive by making false promises
4	lead into	**E**	guide, show the way to
5	lead off with	**C**	start

And now put the above idioms in the correct place.

1. Not having a fixed life pattern will erode the family. That's what it will *lead to*.
2. The speaker *led off* with a survey of the company's objectives.
3. Britain is at the start of a social revolution as it *leads* the world *into* becoming a 24-hour society.
4. Microsoft *leads the field* in software applications.
5. Some travel agencies *lead you on* with their brochures.

Task 4: Wordfinder's corner

Match words from the article with the definitions.

1	list of items to be discussed	E	agenda
2	make stress for people	A	pressurise
3	things to help you to enjoy life	F	entertainment
4	style, rhythm of work	C	work pattern
5	shop open late for buying food	B	off-licence
6	work irregular hours	D	shift work

Find words that have almost the same meaning as those in *italics*.

the report *forecasts* more jobs	the report *predicts* more jobs
employers *put pressure on* workers	employers *pressurise* workers
pubs *close* at midnight	pubs *shut* at midnight
the revolution *gets faster* and *faster*	the revolution *gathers pace*
put social *questions* on the agenda	put social *issues* on the agenda

Find the opposite of the words in *italics*.

a thing of the *future*	a thing of the *past*
numbers *halve* within 10 years	numbers *double* within 10 years
feel *relaxed*	feel *rushed / hectic*
9am	*9pm*

Task 5: Words in context

1. People feel even more *rushed* and hectic.
2. Work *patterns* are changing dramatically.
3. Employers are *pressurising* workers.
4. More people than ever have part-time or *shift work* contracts.

Task 6: Guesswork

1 A, 2 C, 3 C, 4 A, 5 AA, 6 A

Task 7: Scanning for figures

How many people work between 9pm and 11pm?	1000,000
How many people work between 2am and 5am?	300,000
Within how many years will these figures double?	10
How many shoppers tend to shop after 6pm?	25 %

Task 8: Did you get the meaning?

advantages

- more jobs will be created
- you can shop, bank, play etc. around the clock

disadvantages

- people work longer hours
- no fixed working hours
- people do shift work
- people are pressurised by employers
- people live a hectic life, are rushed
- no difference between weekday and weekend

CHAPTER 18

Making both ends meet

Task 1: Scanning for keywords

written agreement between two parties	*contract*
work in the black economy	*moonlighting*
something that is legal	*legitimate*
total number of employees in a company	*workforce*
organisation of workers	*trade union*

Task 2: In other words

She expects us *not to see.*	She expects us *to turn a blind eye.*
These workers here *are not organised.*	These workers here are not in a *trade union.*
I can hardly *live on my salary.*	I can hardly *make ends meet.*
They should *make* some *laws* against this sort of thing.	They should *create* some *legislation* against this sort of thing.
Sabrina is *taking advantage of* us.	Sabrina is *exploiting us.*
She is a *businesswoman.*	She is an *entrepreneur.*

Task 3: Complete the business idioms: One verb – five idioms

turn	a blind eye	ein Auge zudrücken
	over 5 million a year	über 5 Mio pro Jahr umsetzen
	over a new leaf	ein neues Leben beginnen
	up the pressure	den Druck aufrechthalten
	something upside down	etwas auf den Kopf stellen

Task 4: Wordfinder's corner

Find a word that has a similar meaning.

1	van	**D**	Lieferwagen
2	plant	**A**	Fabrik
3	social security	**C**	Sozialversicherung
4	social deductions	**B**	Sozialabgaben
5	income tax	**F**	Einkommensteuer
6	indications	**E**	Anzeichen

Find the verb.

legislation	*legislate*	Gesetz erlassen
exploitation	*exploit*	ausbeuten
contribution	*contribute*	beitragen
security	*secure*	sichern

Task 5: Words in context

1. They pick up workers in *vans* and take them off to farms and factories.
2. Nobody pays any *tax* or *social security.*
3. It is common to find young girls working in textile *plants.*
4. Families know they are being *exploited,* but claim it's better than not working.
5. The company saves on *social contributions* and the worker saves on *income tax.*

Task 6: Guesswork

1 AC, 2 C, 3 B, 4 A

Task 7: Scanning for facts and figures

1. How old are the youngest textile workers?	10 years
2. How much do they earn a day?	$ 5
3. How many percent of the European GDP does the shadow labour market account for?	16 %

Task 8: Scanning for key phrases

Paragraph 1: Nobody pays any tax or social security. The authorities know what is going on.
Paragraph 2: Families know they are being exploited, but claim it's better than not working.
Paragraph 3: Sometimes illegal workers can get more money than their regular colleagues.
Paragraph 4: The Italian government is planning new legislation to allow companies to become legitimate.

CHAPTER 19

Telebusiness from Ireland

Task 1: Scanning for keywords

business by phone	*telebusiness*
advertising and selling by phone	*telemarketing*
market study	market *survey*
phone call free of charge	*toll-free call*

Task 2: In other words

This fish'n chips is *unbelievably* good.	This fish'n chips is *incredibly* good.
I *got my degree* from University College.	*I'm a graduate of* University College.
Your economy is even *growing faster than* the British economy.	Your economy is even *outstripping* the British economy.
It's a *rapidly growing* metropolis.	It's a *sprawling* metropolis.

Task 3: Complete the business idioms

Ron: I was in Ireland last week trying to *set* up a language school. I *made* a call to a real estate agent to check on prices for a building.
Tom: I think you might have *got* a foot in the door three years ago. With the boom in Ireland rents don't *come* as cheap as they used to do.
Ron: Yes, the high cost of living is something you *have* in common with Germany.
Tom: Well, I guess you'll have to invest a lot if you want to *do* business in Ireland.

Task 4: Wordfinder's corner

Find a word that has almost the same meaning as the words in *italics*.

money to motivate the workforce	*incentive*
answer a *question*	answer a *query*
make a call *free of charge*	make a *toll-free* call
show someone's language skills	*indicate* someone's language skills

exceed the demand of linguists	*outstrip* the demand of linguists
a cultural *change*	a cultural *shift*
watch the market carefully	*survey* the market carefully
the market is less *developed*	the market is less *evolved*
having to use the telephone	*being obliged* to use the telephone
create call centres	*set up* call centres

Task 5: Words in context

1. Before you launch a new product you must *survey* the market.
2. A low salary is no *incentive* for workers to do their best.
3. The European Union has *evolved* very slowly.
4. Multilingual graduates answer *queries* and take orders from all over Europe.
5. Flags *indicate* his or her language skills.

Task 6: Guesswork

1 C, 2 C, 3 A, 4 C

Task 7: Scanning for figures

Ireland and the United Kingdom

European call centres now based In Ireland	20 %
New call centres going to Ireland	30 %
UK customers doing business on the phone	70 %

Direct marketing in the USA

Americans buying over the phone every year	$67,000,000
Jobs secured by call centres	$4,000,000
Goods sold over the phone every year	$275,000,000,000

Task 8: Guided note-taking practice

Why are there so many call centres in Ireland?

1. There is a willing workforce.
2. There are many multilingual graduates.
3. American companies have been investing in call centres.
4. The European market is growing rapidly.

CHAPTER 20

Between bulls and bears

Task 1: Scanning for keywords

spend money to make a profit	*invest*
statement about the future	*prediction*
quantity of money given in a single payment	*lump sum*
where the bank keeps your money	*deposit account*
healthy and likely to produce the right result	*sound*

Task 2: In other words

I *made no profit* on my investment.	I got no *return* on investment.
You'd have been better off *investing in various things to reduce* the risk.	You'd have been better off *spreading* the risk.
Variety *guarantees* safety.	Variety *ensures* safety.

Task 3: Complete the business idioms

1. The strike is *spreading to* other companies.
2. The meeting has brought the results we were all *seeking*.
3. We're always *seeking* to improve productivity.
4. We should *spread* our risks. Variety for safety.
5. We will have to *spread* the cost over the year.

Task 4: Wordfinder's corner

A	unit trust (plan)	7	Kapitalanlagevertrag
B	investment trust	6	Investmentgesellschaft
C	tracker fund	5	Aktienindex-Fonds
D	Pep allowances	4	Sparzuschüsse (vom Finanzamt)
E	one off investment	3	einmalige Investition
F	performer	2	Erfolgsaktie
G	savings scheme	1	Sparplan

Task 5: Words in context

Which fund to *choose?*	Which fund to *pick?*
Don't go abroad.	*Stay at home.*
What about a *fund that follows an index?*	What about a *tracker?*
Should you invest through *a savings scheme with tax relief?*	Should you invest through a *Pep?*
Don't *get nervous.*	Don't *panic.*
A strong desire for money is dangerous.	*Greed* is dangerous.
Take your time.	*Be patient.*

Task 6: Guesswork

1 A, 2 C, 3 A, 4 B, 5 CA, 6 B, 7 C

Task 7: Fishing for facts

Are the following statements from the text true (T) or false (F)?

1. If there is a correction of the stockmarket you should sell immediately. **F**
2. It is important to invest a lump sum in a Pep scheme. **F**
3. A tracker fund selects the best shares on the market. **F**
4. If you aren't sure where to invest, pay into an investment fund. **T**

Task 8: Did you get the meaning?

1. The author thinks the investor should (**B**) put his money into various stocks and funds.
2. He is of the opinion you should invest at home because (**B**) it's sometimes difficult to understand what's going on abroad.
3. You needn't panic when there is a correction of the market because you (**B**) have made a long-term investment.

Copyright der Business Press-Artikel

3667/1

Englisch

Uwe Kreisel / Pamela Ann Tabbert
Multilingua Englisch *von Anfang an*
(Buch: rororo 60481 / Buch mit Audio-CD: rororo 60435 / Toncassette: rororo 60482)
English Two *Englisch reden und verstehen. Ein Aufbaukurs*
(Buch: rororo 19320, Toncassette: 19321)
Ultimate Idioms *Der Schlüssel zu den britischen und amerikanischen Redewendungen*
(rororo 18492)
American Slang in letzter Minute *Ein Sprachführer für Kurzentschlossene*
(Buch: rororo 19623 / Buch mit Toncassette: rororo 19624 / Toncassette: rororo 19705)
Lust and Love *English for Flirts. Ein Sprachkurs zum Annähern*
(rororo 19976)

Paul Krieger
Supertrain Grammar *Der direkte Weg zu englischer Grammatik*
(rororo 60107)

Emer O'Sullivan / Dietmar Rösler
Modern Talking *Englisches Quasselbuch mit Sprüchen und Widersprüchen*
(rororo 18427)

rororo sprachen

Ernest Pasakarnis
Master your Idioms *Der Schlüssel zu den englischen Redewendungen*
(rororo 18491)

Christa von Staden
See you later, alligator! *Sprachgewandt mit animalischen Idioms*
(rororo 60367)

Ein Gesamtverzeichnis aller lieferbaren Titel der Reihe *rororo sprachen* finden Sie in der *Rowohlt Revue*. Vierteljährlich neu. Kostenlos in Ihrer Buchhandlung.

Rowohlt im Internet: www.rowohlt.de

Uwe Kreisel
Pamela Ann Tabbert
MultiLingua
Englisch
von Anfang an
mit Audio-CD
rororo
SPRACHEN

Französisch

Französisch lernen: alltagsnah und von Anfang an. Für das Lernen allein oder in der Gruppe.

Claire Bretécher /
Isabelle Jue /
Nicole Zimmermann
Le Français avec les Frustrés
Ein Comic-Sprachhelfer
(rororo 18423)

Béatrice Couzereau
Auf ein Sprichwort! In a byword! En un proverbe! *333 Sprichwörter in drei Sprachen*
(rororo 60274)

Armelle Damblemont /
Petra Preßmar
Multilingua Französisch *von Anfang an*
(Buch: rororo 60477 /
Buch mit Audio-CD:
rororo 60436 /
Toncassette: rororo 60478)

Isabelle Jue /
Nicole Zimmermann
Français Deux *Französisch reden und verstehen. Ein Aufbaukurs*
(Buch: rororo 19311,
Cassette: rororo 19312)
Französisch in letzter Minute
(Buch: rororo 19628 /
Buch mit Toncassette:
rororo 19629 /
Toncassette: rororo 19702)

Ahmed Haddedou
Questions grammaticales de A à Z *Tout ce que vous avez toujours voulu savoir sur la grammaire sans jamais oser le demander*
(rororo 18445)

rororo sprachen

Robert Kleinschroth
La Conversation en s'amusant
Sprechsituationen mit Witz gemeistert
(rororo 18873)

Robert Kleinschroth /
Dieter Maupel
La Grammaire en s'amusant
Wichtige Regeln zum Anlachen
(rororo sprachen 18714)

Marie-Thérèse Pignolo /
Hans-Georg Heuber
Ne mâche pas tes mots *Nimm kein Blatt vor den Mund! Französische Redewendungen und ihre deutschen Pendants*
(rororo 17472)

Jacques Soussan
Pouvez-vous Français?
Programm zum Verlernen typisch deutscher Französischfehler
(rororo 16940)

Rowohlt im Internet:
www.rowohlt.de

3451/5

3452/5